"An encouraging, biblically based journal eve[...] Kelsey walks through the messy yet beautifu[...] faith, tenderness, and wisdom. It's a gentle re[...] girls—you are fearfully and wonderfully made!"

Leslie Means, creator of Her View From Home, *Wall Street Journal* bestselling author of *So God Made a Mother*

"*One Year with Jesus* is an approachable invitation for both introspection and practical application for tweens and teens developing their faith. Kelsey's teaching background shines through and meets girls where they are while pointing them to a path of walking daily with the One who first dreamed them into being."

Jillian Benfield, author of *The Gift of the Unexpected: Discovering Who You Were Meant to Be When Life Goes Off Plan*

"Kelsey's gentle, encouraging spirit shines through in these pages filled with Truth and will speak straight to a girl's heart as she nurtures her own young faith. As a mom of tween and teen girls, I love having this devotional to share with them as they grow."

Carolyn Moore, editor-in-chief, Her View From Home

"*One Year with Jesus* masterfully shines God's Word on real-life issues in to-day's world, bravely addressing heart-level topics that teen girls battle. It's a perfect resource if you're looking to pass your faith to the next generation!"

Jason Drahota, pastor, NorthRidge Church

"*One Year with Jesus* is a deeply needed gift of truth for young teenage girls in a time when so many messages are competing for their attention. Kelsey's guiding words will help them put Jesus right in the center in a way that is relevant to them and will speak directly to their hearts."

Amy Betters-Midtvedt, educator, speaker, writer, and author of *You'll Make It (and They Will Too): Everything No One Talks About When You're Parenting Teens*

"What an honor it is to know and experience Kelsey. Her tireless dedication and unwavering faith shine through every page of this devo curated just for you! Through prayer, study, and passion, she's crafted a guide that reflects her deep love for God and desire to share His truth. Enjoy the journey ahead!"

Grace Current, LCMFT, marriage and family therapist, Restored Counseling

ONE YEAR
with
JESUS

ONE YEAR

with

JESUS

A WEEKLY
Devotional Journal
FOR MIDDLE SCHOOL GIRLS

KELSEY SCISM

BETHANYHOUSE

a division of Baker Publishing Group
Minneapolis, Minnesota

Published by Bethany House Publishers
Minneapolis, Minnesota
BethanyHouse.com

Bethany House Publishers is a division of
Baker Publishing Group, Grand Rapids, Michigan

Printed in the United States of America

Library of Congress Cataloging-in-Publication Data
Names: Scism, Kelsey, author.
Title: One year with Jesus : a weekly devotional journal for middle school girls / Kelsey Scism.
Description: Minneapolis, Minnesota : Bethany House Publishers, a division of Baker Publishing
    Group, [2024] | Includes bibliographical references. | Audience: Ages 11 to 13
Identifiers: LCCN 2023049994 | ISBN 9780764242496 (paper) | ISBN 9781493446735 (ebook)
Subjects: LCSH: Girls—Prayers and devotions—Juvenile literature. | Middle school students—
    Juvenile literature. | Devotional exercises—Juvenile literature. | Christian life—Juvenile
    literature.
Classification: LCC BV4860 .S355 2024 | DDC 242/.62—dc23/eng/20240117
LC record available at https://lccn.loc.gov/2023049994

Cover design by Dan Pitts
Cover illustration by Sarah Kvam
Interior design by William Overbeeke

The author is represented by WordServe Literary Group, WordServeLiterary.com.

Baker Publishing Group publications use paper produced from sustainable forestry practices and postconsumer waste whenever possible.

24   25   26   27   28   29   30   7   6   5   4   3   2   1

For my little sister, Kallie,

whose death strengthened my faith
in ways her living never could have.
I thank God for working *all* things—
even her absence here on earth—
for my good and his glory.

My little sister was eleven years younger than me. I was married and had my first baby when she died at the age of thirteen. Though I was just over a decade older than her, our *faith* age was a lot closer. I didn't understand what it really meant to be a Christian, to follow Jesus, and to have a personal relationship with God until I was in my twenties. Before her death, Kallie was just beginning to understand those things too. So in *faith* age, I'd like to think we were just a few years apart. We had just started to have conversations about God and how he impacted our daily lives.

I didn't get to finish those conversations. It's like they were stopped midsentence. But God continued to plant them in my soul. Deep down, I was filled with words longing to get out, desperate to be used in real conversations with my little sister.

Now, I'm giving those words—those unfinished conversations—to you, my reader. And I kind of feel like you're the little sister God intended them for all along.

Contents

Introduction

A river of changing currents flows between the banks of being a child and being a teenager. It's an awkward place to be. On one bank sits a little girl, and on the other, a young woman—and right now, you find yourself somewhere in between.

In between dressing Barbies and finding your own style. In between beating the boys in a race and imagining what it might be like to go on a date with them. In between childish shows and teen dramas. In between Sunday school coloring sheets and Bible studies. In between singing "Jesus Loves Me" and discovering what that really means.

As a kid, your faith can sometimes feel in-between too. It doesn't really feel like your own—kind of like you're playing dress-up with someone else's clothes, someone else's faith. A faith that belongs to the adults in your life, but every once in a while, you try to put it on and walk around in it. It feels a little awkward and way too big. It doesn't fit you quite right and looks strange hanging in your own closet.

That's because the faith belonging to the adults in your life isn't *yours*. It belongs to them. Sure, we talk about the same God, the same Jesus who loves us and died for us all, and the same Holy Spirit who offers guidance for our souls, but your *faith* is a unique relationship developed over time. And it's yours alone.

If you don't feel that yet, it's okay. We don't wake up one morning and suddenly have a perfectly connected relationship with our Savior. It's built day by day, moment by moment. That's what this book is about. Building your relationship with the Lord. Learning how to see and hear him in your own life. Connecting with God as he pulls you out of the in-between and into your own faith.

I'm excited to be on this journey with you and am looking forward to how God will grow you over this next year. This book is yours—to read, to write in, to make your own—just like your faith. I'm going to offer some suggestions about how to use it.

We're going to talk about self-image, friendships, dating, overwhelming emotions, what it means to be a Christian, how to handle mistakes, and how to walk with Jesus through middle school struggles.

All those topics and more are wrapped up into thirteen overall themes. Within each theme, you'll find four weekly devotionals with journaling space and prayer prompts. The weekly devotionals explore the theme through the categories of God, Self, Relationships, and Living. They will help you discover who God is, who you are, how this affects your relationships, and how to live out your faith.

WEEKLY DEVOTIONAL

- Your week will begin here. Read the verse for the week and the short devotional that goes with it. Feel free to highlight or underline anything that sticks out to you as you read. You can also write notes in the margins: thoughts or questions you have.

- When you're done with the devotional, take out a note card or sticky note and write the week's Scripture verse on it. Then place it somewhere you will see it every day. Making God's Word visible in your daily life is a simple way to connect with him.

QUESTIONS AND JOURNALING SPACE

- There will be three to four questions with each devotional. You can answer all of them at once or one each day.
- These questions are designed to lead you to reflect on what you've read and push you to think more deeply about it and God.
- There are **no wrong answers** to these questions, just your thoughts. You're not being graded. You don't even have to write in complete sentences.

PRAYER PROMPTS

- I could have written a prayer for you and just included it at the end of each week, but that seemed to counteract the purpose of growing your own faith, so instead, I've included prayer prompts. This is the final piece for the week and can be done on its own day after completing the other activities.
- You can write a word-for-word prayer. If you're like me, sometimes writing the exact words helps you to find the words you're looking for. There is no need to worry about proper grammar and accurate spelling. If you choose to write out your prayer, simply write from your heart—that's all that really matters.
- If writing out a word-for-word prayer feels like a lot of work, you can write notes about the specific things you want to cover in your prayer and use them as a guide.
- Or you can simply think through the prayer prompts and pray as you go.
- God doesn't need fancy words and well-constructed sentences. The act of prayer isn't so much about the words; instead, it's about the state of your heart.

OTHER SUGGESTIONS

- Choose the same time each day to work through your activity for the day. Building in consistency will help you establish a routine and stick to it.

- Think about your schedule and which days and times you will be most likely to have time for the devotional. Maybe you have early practice on Mondays, so starting the weekly devotional then won't work well. Maybe you're not an early riser anyway, so mornings aren't a good time for you in general. Maybe you already have a bed-time routine that makes it easy to give ten to fifteen minutes to the devotional.

- Tell someone else the time and day(s) you're committing to reading the devotional—a parent, sibling, friend, youth group leader. Telling someone else kind of forces you to make a commitment to it, and that person can help keep you focused by asking how things are going.

- There is no wrong way to structure your time as long as it works for you.

- It's okay to miss a day. It's okay to get off track with your schedule or make a change. God wants to spend time with you and build your faith. He doesn't love you less if you miss a day. You're not less Christian if you forget to answer a question.

- Finally, enjoy this process of getting to know God better and learning more about who you are and how you can live for Jesus. It is my prayer that through these pages you will develop a personal relationship with our God and Savior and discover a faith that fits perfectly on you.

Who Am I?

I used to be a middle school teacher, and at the beginning of each school year I would guide my middle school students to do an activity titled "Who am I?" Their pages would be filled with words like *daughter*, *sister*, *athlete*, *booklover*, *animal-lover*, *friend*, *hard worker*, and so many others. My goal for the assignment was to get to know my students and give them a creative way to express themselves. There were no right or wrong answers.

Years later, I realized that I failed to teach the *real* lesson. Because there *is* only one right answer to the question "Who am I?" . . . and I hope you find it in the coming pages.

You Are God's Creation

God

> Then the LORD God formed a man from the dust of the ground and breathed into his nostrils the breath of life, and the man became a living being.
>
> Genesis 2:7

My daughter is the definition of creative. Even as a little girl, she was constantly creating something—mostly messes of construction paper, glitter glue, paint, and stickers. Or at least a *mess* is how I viewed it. In her mind, though, she was making masterpieces. I didn't always appreciate her creativity then, but I'm seeing just how great it is now. That messy creativity has turned into a talent for decorating. If it weren't for her, the walls of our home would be bare and plain. And December would look like every other day inside our house but with a Christmas tree.

Home decorating is not my talent. Now, give me some chicken, fresh vegetables, olive oil, seasonings, and some pasta, and I'll make you something delicious. I love standing at the stove top as the aroma from a dish I'm creating makes my stomach growl.

When I create, I require a base of ingredients I can mix together in unique ways to come up with a new dish. A creative artist requires the same base—paints, pencils, clay—ingredients to form a masterpiece. My daughter needs thrift store finds or decor that matches the theme she's dreamed up for a room. Our creativity is revealed as we transform a variety of simple items into something new.

God, however, only needed one thing. Dirt.

That's it. The most basic and lifeless ingredient of all.

"Then the LORD God formed a man from the dust of the ground and breathed into his nostrils the breath of life, and the man became a living being" (Genesis 2:7).

When I read this verse, I imagine a family on a beach building a castle out of sand—filling buckets of water from the ocean, ever so carefully forming towers. Whether the final result is a stunning display of sand architecture or a sand formation that only slightly resembles a crumbling castle, they share one trait . . . they're still just sand and nothing more. Like with dirt, there is no movement, no thoughts, no life within a grain of sand.

When God created the first man, he didn't just mold a life-sized person out of dirt like a sandcastle, he took it one step further. He breathed into his nostrils the breath of life. His creation of dirt became a living, breathing human being—the very first ever.

God's breath created life. Not just any life, but the one life from whom all lives would descend. Isn't that mind-blowing?

Can you imagine breathing onto a canvas and seeing the art you've created come to life? Or whispering breath onto a photo you've just hung on the wall, and suddenly a real, live human stands before you?

How do we even make sense of a God who can form a living being out of dirt?

Our human brains cannot possibly understand what that would be like, no matter how creative our imaginations. That's how awesome God is.

Not only is he the ultimate creative creator, but his breath gives life. We cannot even imagine the power he has. Abilities and characteristics like these help us see just how different God is from us. And when we recognize his power and awesomeness, it leads us to worship him—not because of what he's done but because of who he is.

 Think about it . . .

Many of us hear the word *creative* and immediately shy away, convinced we have no creative talent. But creativity comes in all forms and outlets.

In what ways are you creative (art, cooking, writing, dancing, designing, building, storytelling, acting, decorating, etc.)? Can you think of at least one way you have displayed creativity, even if it's a bit unconventional?

God is the ultimate creator, and his creativity cannot be matched. Step outside for just a few minutes and you'll see what I mean. Seriously, at some point today, spend a few minutes outside—take a walk, sit on the steps outside your home, or even just breathe in some fresh air from an open window. Then spend five minutes simply watching the natural world that surrounds you. (If you can, take this journal with you.) Write down every natural element you see—birds, insects, plants, people, anything not man-made—and be as specific as you can, but don't worry about spelling or getting the exact right name (this isn't a science test).

Look at that list. Think about all the things you saw. What does your list reveal about God's creativity? What can you learn about God from his creation?

> How many are your works, LORD! In wisdom you made them all; the earth is full of your creatures. There is the sea, vast and spacious, teeming with creatures beyond number—living things both large and small.
>
> **PSALM 104:24–25**

How does this verse connect to or support what you've learned about God as a creator this week?

 *Pray about it . . .*

- Tell God what you think about his creativity and power to breathe life into dirt to create a living being.

- Thank him for any unique creative talent he has given you (remember, creativity is more than artistic talent).

- Ask God to help you look for and recognize evidence of his creativity and power all around you.

Deep Down Inside, I'm Like God?

Self

> So God created man in his own image, in the image of God he created him; male and female he created them.
>
> Genesis 1:27 ESV

Have you ever been around a bunch of adults admiring a new baby? After the initial *oohs* and *aahs* and *she's so cutes*, chances are you've heard someone ask, "Who do you think she looks like?" It happens every time. And I should know, I've had a lot of experience—six kids, to be exact. That's six times I've been bombarded by the interrogations, trying to determine who the new baby looks like. My response is usually "I'm not sure. I have such a hard time seeing resemblance like that."

And it's true. Unless I find a baby picture of each sibling and hold it right up next to the new baby's sweet little face, I really can't answer the question.

Our society seems to place a lot of value on who we look like. The Bible talks about this too. Genesis 1:27 tells us we have been made in the image of God. Now, I used to think this meant that the answer to the constantly asked newborn question "Who does she look like?" was simply *God*. She looks like God.

Can you imagine if I told my great-grandma that my baby looks like God? I can almost see the shock on her face and the words sucked right out of her mouth.

But, honestly, for the longest time, I thought that's what this verse meant. That to be made in God's image meant my green eyes, curly hair (which I hated), and long, pointy nose were reflective of God. I thought this verse was referring to my physical features being made in God's image.

It wasn't until recently that I studied this verse and gained a deeper understanding of its meaning. We *are* made in God's image, but this verse is talking about how our souls—who we are at our core—have been made in God's image.

When God breathed life into the first human being, he also breathed life into Adam's soul. A soul created to worship God, a soul designed to reflect God's holiness, a soul made to submit to God's will, a soul made to be filled by God's Spirit.

When the Bible says we've been made in God's image, it's reminding us that the very core of our being is to be like God.

So, since God is holy and righteous, that means we're naturally good, right? Perfect, even? Wrong. We were made in the image of God, but at the same time, we have been born sinful. Just as life entered the world through Adam and Eve in the Garden of Eden, so did sin. And through that first sin, the presence of sin has wrapped itself around our souls.

Imagine a ball about the size of your fist. Inside that ball is a battery pack with an endless supply of power and a lightbulb that never grows dim. The ball glows, shining light from within. But that light isn't always visible to the outside world because the ball is covered in a thick coat of black paint, seemingly impossible for the light to penetrate. That ball of light is your core, made in the image of God. And the thick black paint is sin, surrounding your soul and covering the light it was designed to spread.

But that's not the end of the story. We aren't left to be tossed around through this life—a soul reflecting God's image but covered by sin. You see,

God's own Son chose to become a man and live on this earth. He chose to become the final sacrifice for sin—yours and mine. Through his death and resurrection, he restored our relationship with God, our creator. When he rose from the grave after three days in the tomb, something happened to our souls.

That thick black paint covering the ball of endless light began to crack. Because of God's grace and forgiveness, the light shines through those cracks, revealing tiny streams of light breaking through.

Our souls, made in God's image, are not trapped forever by the thick darkness of sin. God made a way—through Jesus—for our souls to do what they were designed to . . . reflect him and shine his light into the world.

When you put your faith in him—a decision only you can make—that dark coating begins to crack. And one day, when you're reunited with the creator of your soul in heaven, every last flake of that black paint will be washed away and your soul will only be light, just as it was designed, made in God's image.

 Think about it . . .

How does the illustration of a ball of light covered by thick black paint help you understand what it means to be made in God's image while also being born a sinner?

If sin had never entered the world, how do you think your life would be different? What would your life be like if your core being, your soul, had never been impacted by sin? How would it change the way you act? The things you say? The way you treat others?

> All of us, like sheep, have strayed away. We have left God's paths to follow our own. Yet the LORD laid on him [Jesus] the sins of us all.
>
> ISAIAH 53:6 NLT

How does this verse connect to or support what you've learned about yourself this week?

 # Pray about it . . .

- Tell God what it means to you to be made in his image.

- Admit to him that your soul is covered by sin and you struggle to follow him in all you do.

- Thank him for sending Jesus as the final sacrifice for sin and offering you forgiveness.

- Ask God to help you chip away at the thick, dark paint of sin that covers your soul by recognizing when you do wrong and asking for forgiveness so that his light inside your soul can shine through.

God Made Me . . . and Her

Relationships

> Make every effort to live in peace with everyone and to be holy;
> without holiness no one will see the Lord.
>
> Hebrews 12:14

Can I confess something to you? Sometimes people drive me nuts. I know—I'm a mom, an adult, a Christian woman—I'm not supposed to dislike people. That confession doesn't sound very Christlike, but it's true. There are certain people who just feel hard to love.

And since we're being honest, can you think of someone who drives you nuts? Maybe it's a sibling, your mom or dad, a certain teacher, or (even more likely) a girl your age. That one person who gets under your skin, resulting in you lashing out, talking poorly about them behind their back, or getting downright mad at them.

I call these people the But-Shes in my life because when I get frustrated with them and react accordingly, my initial response is "But she (or he) . . ."

But she said some awful things about me.

But she ruined my favorite sweatshirt.

But she's so controlling.

But she keeps doing such stupid things.

But she lied.

But she's so annoying.

But she is the meanest person I know.

When we encounter a But-She, we always seem able to justify our reactions and treatment of her with something *she's* done. We feel like whatever we've done to her isn't nearly as bad as what she first did to us.

Remember last week when we talked about our core being—our soul—being made in God's image? That truth applies to her too. Her soul is made in God's image. Kind of hard to hear, isn't it? It's so much easier to dislike someone when you think of her as the enemy.

However, when you recognize that not only is she *not* the enemy, but she (like you) is made in God's image, God starts to soften your heart toward your But-She. It's not easy, and it doesn't happen immediately, but as you begin to view these people who frustrate you as people made in God's image, enveloped by a sinful nature, your attitude toward them shifts.

Our verse this week doesn't tell us to become best friends with these people who drive us nuts, but it does tell us to live at peace with them. Furthermore, it tells us to be holy. Now, we've already established that sin keeps us from being perfect and holy (Jesus was the only perfect human), but that doesn't mean we can't approach this person with a desire to interact with them out of God's holiness. We cannot accomplish this on our own. We must rely on God when our frustration and annoyance threaten to result in unholy behavior.

How exactly do we live in peace, guided by holiness, when we are stuck with people who drive us nuts? Through prayer and reliance on God.

Before you find yourself in an encounter with your But-She, knowing it will likely lead to emotions of frustration, annoyance, and anger . . . pray. Tell God you're concerned about spending time with this person, and ask him for peace in advance. Ask him to guide your words, actions, and reactions.

In the middle of an interaction with this person, when negative emotions have already begun to bubble up and you find yourself on the verge of lashing out . . . pray. Ask God to soften your heart and open your eyes to see the person as someone made in his image. Ask him to replace your negative emotions with his peace toward her in that very moment.

After you walk away from time with your But-She, thinking back on your words and actions . . . pray. Ask God to show you ways in which you failed to show holiness, and then ask for forgiveness. Thank him for the ways he showed up and helped you stay calm despite your initial emotions of frustration, annoyance, and anger.

Praying before, through, and after these situations connects us to God, giving him space to work through us in his strength when we don't have the willpower to control our emotions and interactions on our own.

It's not like in school when the teacher hands you a test but refuses to help you with a problem, reminding you that it's a test and you have to figure it out on your own. That's not how God works. Instead, he hands you the test and holds your hand through it, leading and guiding you the whole time. You simply have to ask him for help through prayer.

Isn't he a great God?

✳ Think about it . . .

Who are the But-Shes in your life?

Now, copy these words, filling in the blank with her (or his) name:
So God created _____ in his own image, in the image of God he created _____. Repeat the sentence for each person listed above.

How does being reminded that these people are made in God's image impact your view of them?

> A new commandment I give to you, that you love one another: just as I have loved you, you also are to love one another. By this all people will know that you are my disciples, if you have love for one another.
>
> **JOHN 13:34–35 ESV**

How does this verse connect to or support what you've learned about dealing with people you don't like this week?

 # Pray about it . . .

- Tell God what it means to you that he doesn't give instructions and leave you to carry them out by yourself.

- Thank him for loving you even when you don't act lovable.

- Ask him to show you any relationships that need more attention when it comes to living at peace with others.

- Admit that your words, actions, and reactions don't always reflect the holiness of God, and ask him for forgiveness for those times.

- Ask him to guide your relationships and to help you live in peace with everyone—even those you don't necessarily like.

Becoming Who God Created You to Be

Living

> "For I know the plans I have for you," declares the LORD, "plans to prosper you and not to harm you, plans to give you hope and a future."
>
> Jeremiah 29:11

When I was in high school, many days at lunch we played this sort of game—I called it "What should Kelsey be when she grows up?" I'd sit at the table, brainstorming career options with my friends. My list included but wasn't limited to a pediatric nurse practitioner (I even did a research paper on that one), something to do with running a restaurant, anything that didn't involve math (spoiler alert: almost *everything* involves math), a journalist, and even a speech writer for the president. You know what wasn't on my list? A teacher. I refused to add it. There was no way I was going to be a teacher.

Until I was.

I entered college as a communications major. I had no idea what I was going to do with that degree, but it sounded like a good plan at the time. However, it wasn't God's plan.

In the first months of my freshman year of college, while working at a sporting goods store, I sat next to my boss's son, who was working on his English homework. I folded T-shirts for a screen-printing order and helped him as he worked. I don't remember what the assignment was about, but I remember being overcome by a thought that wouldn't leave me alone—I was meant to be a teacher.

By second semester, I was an education major.

I grew up being told I could be anything I wanted to be. You know, the if-you-can-dream-it-you-can-do-it mindset. But here's the problem. I *couldn't* be anything I wanted to be. No matter how much I wanted to be a communications major, that wasn't God's plan for me. And I'm forever grateful he changed my stubborn heart that insisted I would NEVER be a teacher.

I'm wondering if you've been told that you can be anything you want to be. The phrase is often spoken with good intentions, with a desire to inspire and encourage you. But I don't agree with it.

You can't be anything you want. But you can be everything God has created you to be.

You see, the be-anything-you-want mentality forgets that God has created each of us for a unique purpose, and outside of that purpose, we won't feel truly fulfilled.

Now, you have several years before you need to make decisions about college and careers, but it's not too early to start praying about the future. In fact, I bet you've already been asked what you want to be when you grow up. Maybe someone has told you that you can be anything you want to be. Maybe you already have dreams about your future. Or maybe you're like high school me and feel a little lost and confused about what you want to be.

As you brainstorm careers and dreams, I hope you'll remember that God has a plan for you, a plan to use you and the unique characteristics, skills, and talents he's created in you, a plan to bring him glory, a plan to fill your soul with purpose.

This isn't meant to scare you away from dreaming big. It's meant to help you begin the process of involving God in your future plans. It's meant to show you the importance of inviting God into your dreams—dreams that can come true when they match up with God's will for you and the plan he has for your life.

Some of my biggest dreams (writing this book, for example) would never have happened—maybe not even have ever been dreamed of—if it weren't for God's leading. Becoming an author was *never* on my career list. What I didn't realize sitting around that high school cafeteria lunch table was that the plan God had for me was so much better than my own.

I want you to have big dreams that display God's glory and follow his plan for your life.

So, instead of striving to be whatever you *want* to be . . . strive to be who God has created you to be.

 Think about it . . .

If you could be anything you wanted to be, what would you be? Do you think this matches with who God created you to be? Why or why not?

Can you think of someone you know who seems to be exactly what they want to be *and* who God created them to be? How do you know they're both?

What would it look like for you to involve God in your plans for the future and invite him into your dreams?

> **Then you will call on me and come and pray to me, and I will listen to you. You will seek me and find me when you seek me with all your heart.**
>
> JEREMIAH 29:12–13

How does this verse connect to or support what you've learned about God and dreams? Notice that these verses directly follow the verse about God having a plan for your life. How do they connect?

Pray about it . . .

- Thank God for having a plan for your life.

- Tell him how amazing it is that he has created each of us with a specific purpose.

- Admit that you sometimes dream without involving him in your dreams.

- Ask him to help you have dreams that match up with who he's created you to be and to show you what those dreams are.

I'm Not Good Enough

I'm willing to bet chore money that you've said these words before. *I'm not good enough to make the team, I'm not good enough to be her friend, I'm not a good enough daughter or sister.*

I grew up saying these words, or ones similar to them, and it wasn't until Jesus chased me down and gave me hope that I came to realize that being good enough isn't actually about me.

In the next four weeks, we'll explore what it means to be good and why it matters.

And It Was Good

God

God saw all that he had made, and it was very good. And there was evening, and there was morning—the sixth day.

Genesis 1:31

Summer is great, isn't it? No school, sunshine, afternoons at the pool, vacations. I mean, what's not to love?

Actually, there is one thing not to love—the bugs. With summer comes bugs . . . at least where I live. Flies, ants, spiders, moths, June bugs, and mosquitoes. Mosquitoes are the worst.

Have you ever had a mosquito bite? You know those annoying little bumps that itch like crazy and then turn red and sometimes scab over when you itch them too much? After you've been bitten, it's an endless cycle of itch and scratch. It's easy to notice a mosquito bite when you have one, but have you ever looked closely at the mosquito?

Of course you haven't because they're tiny and fly off the moment you try to smack them. Or, if you are successful at smacking one mid-bite, they get smashed into a smear, leaving no chance to examine the little creature.

If you did have a chance to examine them, you'd find their bodies are made up of the head, thorax, and abdomen, together containing eleven distinct parts, including a reproductive and respiratory system.

It's kind of crazy, isn't it? Those tiny little bugs have complex systems designed not only to keep them alive but to reproduce, populating the earth with more buzzing, biting creatures.

Each time I start to think about how *bugged* I am by these insects, I am reminded that they are part of God's creation. And all of God's creation is good—even mosquitoes. I'm still not sure why they're here or what kind of good purpose they serve, but I know God created them and he thinks they are good . . . because that's what he says in his Word. It's all good. Every single thing he created—God saw all that he had made, and it was good.

When I think of a mosquito, the last word I would use to describe it is *good*.

Pesky? Yes.

Stupid? Probably.

Useless? Uh-huh.

Worthless? I think so.

And yet, God looks at that mosquito and calls it good.

We assign the term *good* to things we place value in. Maybe your lunch today was good. You got a good grade on your last quiz. When your parents ask how your day was, *good* is a safe, no-need-for-more-discussion kind of answer.

But when we look at the word *good* in the creation story, it has a little more power. God assigns the term *good* to all he created not because they have value or worth on their own, but because *he* created them. We don't get to decide whether or not God's creation is good because he has already declared it as that. *Pesky, stupid, useless, worthless*—these words reflect the value *we* have given to the mosquito, but in God's eyes that creature is good because his creation is good.

When I get to heaven, I think I'm going to ask God about that . . . why exactly did you create the mosquito? Now that I think about it, I have a whole list of creatures I might ask him about. Sticking with insects, I'd like to know the purpose of flies and gnats too. Or what about a sloth? Other than turning them into cute cartoon-like stickers, do they *do* something? Eww, or what about the naked mole rat? Surely God can't think that creature is good?

Yet I believe God's Word to be true, so I must also believe that all he created is, indeed, good . . . even that mosquito. We don't need to see or understand the goodness of something to accept the value God has given it. Maybe that's part of God's goodness—to see value and worth where we can't.

 **Think about it . . .**

Did you know, according to the CDC:

> There are over 3,700 types of mosquitoes found throughout the world.
>
> Adult mosquitoes live two to four weeks, depending on external factors.
>
> Only female mosquitoes bite to get a blood meal. The male's proboscis (think needle-like mouth part) is not strong enough to pierce skin.
>
> Mosquitoes use their antennae to detect carbon dioxide from a person's breath or air movement.
>
> A mosquito can stand and walk on water.[1]

Did you learn something today? All kinds of useless facts about mosquitoes, right? Put a star next to the one you thought was most interesting. Why did that one stick out to you?

If you were to look up a detailed diagram of a mosquito, you would find at least ten unique body parts identified. In general, mosquitoes are less than half of an inch—no bigger than your fingernail. And yet, they have specific body parts designed for unique uses that make them able to do things other animals can't. These tiny bugs are another example of God's creativity and purposeful design. If God gave this much attention to designing a pesky insect, what does that tell you about his thoughts when designing *you*?

Write about how it makes you feel to know that God created both the mosquito and you . . . and that he considers everything he has made to be very good.

> Ah, Sovereign Lord, you have made the heavens and the earth by your great power and outstretched arm. Nothing is too hard for you.
>
> JEREMIAH 32:17

How does this verse connect to or support what you've learned about God as a creator this week?

 Pray about it . . .

- Tell God how awesome he is for considering every little detail as he created the world and everything in it.

- Ask God to show you things in your life that you have assigned value to based on your view of them.

- Admit that you don't always see God's creation as good and forget that it has value simply because he created it.

- Ask God to prepare your heart to see all of his creation as good.

What If I Don't Like Me?

Self

And so we know and rely on the love God has for us. God is love.
Whoever lives in love lives in God, and God in them.

1 John 4:16

Too fat. Too skinny. Too loud. Too quiet. Too awkward. Too shy. Too short. Too tall. Too dark. Too pale. Too dumb. Too nerdy. Too simple. Too needy. Too . . . *me.*

Do you ever have days when you don't like yourself and have trouble believing anyone else could ever like you? Not even God. The list of all the things you dislike about yourself plays like an annoying song stuck in your head, and no matter what you do, you can't seem to turn it off.

On those days when you don't like yourself, it's really hard to believe that God could possibly like you. You're obviously too much for him, a hopeless case.

But if I google "Bible verses about how much God loves you," one of the first results that pops up shows forty different verses. God's Word makes it abundantly clear—he *loves* you. And this love isn't dependent on you. This love doesn't change because of your behavior or his mood. You are not *too anything* to prevent God from loving you . . . *love* is who he is.

We've been talking about creation a lot so far. We've already said that you are God's creation, made in his image. And we've talked about how God looked at all he had made (even the mosquito) and declared it was good. Very good.

So what does this mean for you? It means that as God's creation, he has declared that you are good.

Now, unfortunately, Satan (who, by the way, is very real—we'll talk about that later) doesn't want you to believe that God loves you. He doesn't want you to see yourself as a very good creation. He would much rather you get stuck in the endless cycle of too this or too that because it distracts you from the truth of God's Word. He wants you to feel unlikeable because that makes his job easier, and his job is to fill you with lies so you don't have room for God's truth.

Okay, that's great, you're thinking, *Satan = lies and God = truth. But how does that help me when I really, honestly, deep down inside don't like myself?*

And this is the part where I wish I was sitting on your bed next to you. I wish I could hand you a tissue as the tears fall down your cheeks and you whisper between breaths and release the pain of admitting that you don't like yourself. Because it's right then that I would take your hand, squeeze it tightly, and say, "You don't have to like yourself for God to love you."

God's love isn't dependent on your feelings. He created you and calls you good—very good—no matter how you feel about yourself.

So will you try something for me? A little experiment. I'm even okay with a *fine, I don't think this will work, but I'll try it because you asked me to* kind of effort.

Will you replace Satan's lies with God's truth? Will you rely on his love (as our verse today tells us) and not your own feelings?

Every time (and I mean *every* time) one of those nasty too-something thoughts pops into your brain, will you stop yourself and whisper these words:

God created me, and he calls me good. I don't have to like myself for God to love me.

Maybe you could even write these words down on a sticky note and stick it on your planner, your locker, your bedroom nightstand, or your bathroom mirror. Write them on your hand for all I care (maybe ask a parent about that one first—don't get me in trouble here, okay?). Wherever and however you choose to do it, make these words visible and a part of your internal vocabulary.

Rely on God's love, and start choosing his truth over Satan's lies.

 ## Think about it . . .

Maybe it's not just your internal voice speaking all the things you don't like about yourself. Maybe you've actually heard those words spoken about you or to you. Maybe a friend, in a sort of joking way, made a comment that has stuck with you. Maybe a brother or sister knows exactly which button to push when it comes to mean comments and has pushed the same one so many times that you now believe the words. Maybe an adult in your life has said something that makes it hard to like yourself.

What would it look like to stand up for yourself, not just to yourself, but to that person as well? What would it feel like to say out loud, "You don't have to like me for God to love me"? You don't actually have to say those words to those people, but write about what that might look like, feel like, sound like in the space below. Maybe even write out the exact words you would say to that person.

God didn't mass-produce human beings like American Girl dolls. He could have. But he didn't. Instead, he has chosen to uniquely create each and every human being on this earth so that no two look or act or think exactly the same way.

At the time I am writing this, according to Google, there are more than eight billion people in the world. That's 8,000,000,000 plus!!!

What does this fact make you think about God?

.

> For you created my inmost being; you knit me together in
> my mother's womb. I praise you because I am fearfully and
> wonderfully made; your works are wonderful, I know that full well.
>
> PSALM 139:13–14

How does this verse connect to or support what you've learned about yourself this week?

 # Pray about it . . .

- Tell God how awesome he is to create each human as a unique being, unlike any other.

- Admit that you sometimes struggle to like yourself, and ask him to forgive you for doubting his creation skills and his love.

- Ask him to help you like yourself more and to fight the lies from Satan by replacing them with his truth.

- Admit that you cannot do it on your own.

- Thank him for making you and for calling you good.

PS: It is common for a girl your age to struggle with liking herself, but these thoughts shouldn't consume you or make you wonder if your life is worth living. If you feel like you are drowning in self-hatred, have considered hurting yourself, or have thought about ways you could end your life, tell someone you trust about these thoughts and ask them to help you. God does not want to see you suffer like this, and he has put people around you who can help. He created counselors, therapists, and doctors with unique skills and a passion for helping us take care of our mental health. It's okay to ask for their help.

What If Other People Don't Like Me?

Relationships

When I am afraid, I put my trust in you. In God, whose word I praise—in God I trust and am not afraid. What can mere mortals do to me?

Psalm 56:3–4

I'm going to admit something to you that sounds kind of weird. Sometimes I am jealous of animals. I know there are lots of things about animal life that I would never want to experience: I don't want to live outside. I think licking myself clean sounds disgusting. And dry dog food is not a delicacy I want on my plate.

It's not what animals *have* that triggers a hint of jealousy in my heart, it's what they *don't* have. You see, God created animals differently than humans—they aren't made in God's image. They don't have emotions like we do.

I'm jealous of them because animals don't feel lasting things in response to what's been said to them.

A polar bear has never been told her fur isn't white enough. A cow has never been called fat by another cow. A mouse has never felt belittled because she was called dumb. It doesn't matter what family a bird comes from because no one has ever told her that her family is trash.

But when someone makes these kinds of comments to us, it hurts. It hurts deeply.

There are times when we might choose sleeping outside or eating worms instead of feeling the way we do when someone questions our worth. Those times when someone makes us feel so unlovable that we start to believe them.

You know what I'm talking about, don't you? In fact, a comment someone has made to you might have already pounded its way into your mind. A comment made by a brother or sister, a classmate, or maybe even an adult—these people are mere mortals, humans with an earthly beginning and end, beings who are born sinful. But when people speak nasty things to you, especially if the same comment is made over and over, it's really hard not to believe it. Convincing yourself that what they've said isn't true is much harder than it sounds. But what if instead of trying to convince yourself their words *aren't* true, you considered what *is* true. What if you put your trust in God and his truth?

When someone speaks ugliness into your life, I want you to talk to yourself. Seriously, I do. I want you to have the following one-way conversation with yourself. If you're alone, speak the words aloud. If you're surrounded by others, whisper them in your heart.

Does (insert name) determine my worth?
No. (Name) does not determine my worth.
Who does determine my worth?
God.
What does God say about me?
*He says I am fearfully and wonderfully made **by him**.*
He says he loves me so much he sent his Son to die for me.
He says that even when I feel alone, drowning in awful words others have said to me, he is with me.

Have this conversation with yourself every time someone else's words try to make you feel unworthy. I want you to say them so much that you memorize them without even trying. In the back of this book, you'll find a page with the words to take with you on it. Cut it out and keep it somewhere it will be easy to get to when you get attacked by nasty words: put it in your backpack, planner, or pencil box; tape it to your mirror; use it as a bookmark; keep it in your gym locker.

Words to Take with You

God determines my worth.
I am fearfully and wonderfully made.

God loves me so much he sent
his only Son to die for me.

He says that even when I feel alone,
he is with me.

As I write this, I'm praying for you. I'm praying that God will use the words above to touch your heart and that you will feel his love. I'm praying that his voice of love will drown out all the mean things people have said about you and that you will feel the worth he has created in you.

✳ Think about it . . .

People use words as a weapon to hurt you, to tear you down, to make you feel unworthy. But God's got a bigger weapon—that of his love. Nothing, not even death, can separate you from his love. But maybe you can separate yourself from the people who are unkind to you. Can you think of any ways to avoid them? Maybe that means putting physical distance between you: not hanging out together anymore, avoiding places they regularly are, or not sitting near them. Maybe it means putting emotional distance between you: not following them on social media, deleting them as a contact on communication apps. I know this distance isn't always possible, but what would it look like to separate yourself from that person?

People use mean words as weapons. God uses his love as a weapon. And you can use what the Bible says as a weapon. In the space below, I want you to write down mean words that have been said to you or about you. Then I want you to cross those words out and write a truth from God's Word beside them. If you're not sure what God's Word says about you, start with one of these: God loves me. God created me. God thinks I'm valuable.

This week, instead of looking at another verse, I want you to listen to a song—"Mean Girls" by Leanna Crawford. Listen to the whole song and then answer the question below.

How does this song connect to or support what you've learned about yourself, God, and people who are mean to you?

 Pray about it . . .

- Tell God about the words and people who have hurt you. Explain how they make you feel.

- Ask him to help you feel his love and remind you of your worth.

- Thank him for giving you the Bible, where you can find truth about your worth so you don't have to base it on other people's opinions of you.

I Can Be Confident because of What God Says about Me

Living

> Are not two sparrows sold for a penny? Yet not one of them will fall to the ground outside your Father's care. And even the very hairs of your head are all numbered. So don't be afraid; you are worth more than many sparrows.
>
> Matthew 10:29–31

I want you to take a little field trip today. Put this book down and go find your hairbrush. Go ahead, go get it, and bring it back here. If you have curly hair and don't brush your hair, like me, grab a recently used ponytail holder. (PS: Straight-haired girls, we're not gross . . . it's just that brushing our hair pulls out the curl, so we don't use brushes, maybe a wide-toothed comb. If you know, you know.)

Sorry, I got distracted. Did you get your brush or ponytail holder? Good.

Now, clean it. Pull out all the hairs from the brush or elastic. And count them. Lay them out one by one and count them. I'll wait.

How'd that go? How many hairs did you count? Ten or twenty? Fifty? Over a hundred? Or did you lose track? Or maybe you looked at that pile of a tangled mess and just gave up. Counting the number of hairs left behind in your brush or ponytail holder is a nearly impossible task, isn't it? Can you imagine trying to count each hair on your head? Ridiculous, right?

But God knows. He knows the exact number of hairs on your head at any given moment. They are numbered. And that means he knows how many you lose each time you brush it, wash it, or pull out those elastic rubber bands. He *still* knows the number.

Okay. Another question. Do you know how many dollars you have in your bank account or purse or mason jar or piggy bank or envelope—wherever you keep money? Do you think your parents know how many dollars are in their bank account?

If you take the money a person has, plus the dollar value of the things they own, and subtract any debts they have, you'll find that person's net worth. A Google search says that Jeff Bezos (the founder of Amazon) has a net worth of more than 150 billion dollars, and Elon Musk (the SpaceX guy) is worth more than 240 billion dollars. Taylor Swift (I think you know who she is) now has a reported net value of over 1 billion dollars.[1]

If you could count the hairs in your brush as dollars, you still wouldn't be able to compare to the net worth of these people. But you know what? You and Jeff and Elon and even Taylor have the same net worth in God's eyes.

In Matthew 10, when Jesus tells us that even the hairs on our heads are numbered, he's making a point about our net worth. He also talks about the sparrow—it took *two* of them to equal the value of a single penny. Yet God considered the sparrow valuable: not *one* would fall to the ground outside his care (Matthew 10:29). God gives individual attention to each of the millions of sparrows on this earth, and he deems you more important than many.

Do you see how important you are to your Heavenly Father? God cares about the sparrow falling to the ground, and he cares even more about you— your daily activities, your troubles, and your successes . . . even the number of hairs on your head—because you are valuable to him. Jesus defined your worth as priceless when he chose to die on the cross for you. If Jesus attributes such great worth to you, shouldn't you do the same for yourself?

It's so easy to question your worth, especially when you start comparing it to those around you. She's more athletic. She's prettier. Her family has more money. She has nicer things. She's smarter. She's more popular.

But, girl, your worth isn't determined by her or what she has. It's determined by God and what he has done for you. And *that* is where you can find your confidence.

 Think about it . . .

Name a person you think shows confidence. What about that person displays confidence? What do you think he or she is confident in?

As a believer in God, your confidence comes from a unique place. This is incredibly important when it comes to having confidence. Notice I didn't say *self*-confidence. I didn't say the confidence other people have in you. As Christians, we have a far more powerful confidence to lean on (especially when our self-confidence is low or the confidence of others in us isn't obvious). We have *God*-confidence.

This confidence doesn't come from your skills or abilities . . . it comes from knowing God can use you for his glory.

It doesn't come from your physical looks . . . it comes from knowing God created your inmost being in his image.

It doesn't come from other people who tell you all the good things about you . . . it comes from God telling you that you are worthy to him.

How might God-confidence change the way you see yourself? Change the way you act? Change the way you react to other people's opinions of you?

> But blessed is the one who trusts in the LORD, whose confidence is in him. They will be like a tree planted by the water that sends out its roots by the stream. It does not fear when heat comes; its leaves are always green. It has no worries in a year of drought and never fails to bear fruit.
>
> JEREMIAH 17:7–8

How does this verse connect to or support what you've learned about having confidence this week?

 # Pray about it ...

- Thank God for the way he loves you and cares for you and sees you.

- Admit that your confidence often relies on your own opinions or those of others.

- Tell him about the areas in your life where you struggle to have confidence and ask him to help you see yourself through his eyes.

- Ask God to help you grow in God-confidence, trusting that he created you, can use you, and sees worth in you.

I Don't Like What I See in the Mirror

Raise your hand if you love every aspect of your physical appearance.

Wait. You didn't raise your hand.

Raise your hand if you dislike some aspects of your physical appearance.

Mm-hmm. I see those hands.

You know what? You're not alone. I have never met a middle school girl who looks in the mirror each morning and says, "Man, I love this. Look. At. Me. I am a 10. Maybe even a 12."

And if I can be real for just a second, I don't know many grown women who feel that way either.

And you know what else? I'm not even sure that it's possible to love every aspect of your physical appearance. But I am sure that you and I need to *appreciate* our bodies and accept the truth about them. That's what we'll focus on for the next four weeks.

Females Are a Unique Creation

God

> So God created human beings in his own image. In the image of
> God he created them; male and female he created them.
>
> Genesis 1:27 NLT

If I put a newborn girl and a newborn boy side by side with only their diapers on, do you think you could tell the difference? Would their eyes indicate male or female? What about their toes? Or the amount of hair? None of these things at the very basic level, that of a newborn, indicate male or female.

Now, if we remove their diapers, things would get obvious. Even at birth, God created males and females differently. Actually, it happened way before they were born, but that's a different discussion.

We've already talked about how Genesis 1:27 says that you, at your core, are made in God's image. Notice that in the same verse God explains that we are made in his image, he also explains that he created humans as male and female. Though your body was not created in God's image, he was intentional about the way it was formed.

My point is this: you have been uniquely created as a female, which means your body can do some pretty amazing things that a boy's cannot. Don't worry, I'm not going to go into details—I'll leave that lesson for health class and your parents. But I do want you to think about the way God has uniquely created us: male and female.

You see, God created our female bodies in such a unique and intentional way. He created them to conceive life, carry life, and deliver life. You and I, as females, have life-giving bodies.

Think about that for a minute. The body knit together inside your mother's womb, the body born as a crying infant, the body incapable of controlling its own functions—*that* body came into this world designed to generate life.

The size of that body, its hair color, or the shape of its nose had *no* impact on its life-giving functions. Our society places value on our exterior, but God determines value based on the interior—that innermost place created in his image.

So, girls, even when we cannot *love* our bodies, can we switch our focus to appreciating them simply because God made them?

Can we appreciate them not for their shape or size but because God created them uniquely to do things only females can do?

Can we appreciate them because God created our bodies to have physical differences from boys that make us obviously female?

Can we appreciate that our bodies literally carry us through life, that they give us the ability to move and feel and experience physical sensation?

Can we appreciate the amazing creation of our bodies and love God for the work he has done?

It's easy to pick apart our bodies and point out all our flaws, to make a list of all the things we don't like. But when we engage in that behavior, we are picking apart God's creative talents. We are essentially saying to God, "You got this wrong."

God created our bodies—our female bodies—with intention. Let's stop looking at them with critical eyes and instead see ourselves as God's creation. And let's thank God for the good work he has done.

✻ Think about it ...

What is the one part of your body you dislike the most? For me, it's been my nose—it's long and skinny and seems to stick out from my face just a little too far. Anytime I see someone with a cute, diamond-studded nose ring, I get a little jealous and think, *That would look awful on me; it would just draw attention to my big nose.*

We all have aspects of our body we're not in love with. I'm not trying to force you to *love* your body—I want you to *appreciate* it. Can you think for just a second about what you could appreciate about that unliked part? My big nose allows me to smell. Because of it, I am transported back to my grandma's kitchen each time I smell freshly baked bread. Because of it, I am warned of danger, like smoke in the air or a strange smell of gas.

Though I'm not to a place where I can say I love my nose, I can appreciate it. Can you do the same? Write down your least favorite part of your body and then list at least two things you can appreciate about it.

Do you think about breathing? What about blinking? Or walking down the hallway? Do you have to intentionally think about any of those things and command your body to do them? No. They just happen. Because God designed so much of our bodies to function in the background without having to be told to do so.

List ten things your body does for you in a day. Think about physical movement, what's going on inside your body (i.e., respiratory or digestive systems), and how it allows you to interact with others.

> **I will sing to the Lord as long as I live. I will praise my God to my last breath! May all my thoughts be pleasing to him, for I rejoice in the Lord.**
>
> PSALM 104:33–34 NLT

How does this verse connect to or support what you've learned about your body and God?

 *Pray about it . . .*

- Thank God for creating your body uniquely female.

- Tell him three specific things you appreciate about your body.

- Admit that you don't always praise his creation but instead complain about it.

- Ask God to help shift your focus from what you hate about your body toward things you can appreciate. Ask him to help you see his design work in you.

Why Should I Take Care of My Body?

Self

Do you not know that your bodies are temples of the Holy Spirit, who is in you, whom you have received from God? You are not your own; you were bought at a price. Therefore honor God with your bodies.

1 Corinthians 6:19–20

I wasn't made to clean my room as a kid. We lived in an old two-story farmhouse—our bedrooms were upstairs, and my parents' room, the kitchen, bathroom (the only one), and living areas were on the main floor. Once we reached an age that we put ourselves to bed, our parents rarely came up to our rooms. Therefore, our rooms could be as clean or as messy as we wanted, and they'd never even know.

Sounds like a dream, doesn't it?

Cleaning and organizing my room weren't high on my priority list, so I rarely did either. Then one day, I'd need a specific shirt or a pair of jeans to wear to school but couldn't find them in my dresser. So I'd be forced to dig around through the clothes scattered all over my floor (some clean, some dirty—hard to know which) to find that specific item.

Can I just tell you that not having to clean my room wasn't nearly as dreamy as it sounds?

Also, I need to mention that my messiness wasn't the fault of my parents. They gave me the responsibility of keeping my room clean—I'm the one who failed to accept it. And, for the record, I tell (okay, maybe nag) my kids to clean their own rooms today.

While you may grumble your way through the chore of cleaning, ultimately, I hope you understand that it feels better to live in a space that is cleaned regularly. Just as we need to keep our living areas neat and clean, so must we do with our bodies. Although God has created our bodies, we must maintain them.

Everyday hygiene is obviously important: bathing, brushing teeth, combing hair, wearing deodorant, etc. These daily routines allow our physical appearance to reflect cleanliness. This honors God by showing him that we are taking care of the gift he's given us.

Paying attention to what we put into our bodies is also critical. Choosing foods that provide the body with the necessary energy for daily operations. Rejecting dangerous methods for losing weight, like self-induced vomiting, starvation, or excessive exercise. Avoiding unhealthy substances like drugs and alcohol. All of these things are important for maintaining our physical temples in which the Holy Spirit lives.

Setting aside time for movement is also important. You don't have to commit to the most recent exercise trend to be healthy. Remember, we are working to appreciate the way God designed our bodies, and he designed us to move. This might mean going for a walk and listening to music, playing a game of tag with a younger sibling, offering to walk the dog or play fetch with him, dancing, etc. Incorporating movement into your routine honors God by using your body the way he created it to be used.

While movement is important, so is rest. Your body and mind need sleep to recharge and prepare for the upcoming day. Committing to giving your body rest honors God by acknowledging that he created you with a need for sleep. So put down the book, turn off your phone, hit the power button on the TV, click the lights off, and rest like God created you to.

Your body is a temple of the Holy Spirit—the room in which he lives—so it's important to keep that room clean. Honor God with your body by caring for it well so that God can use you in ways that honor him.

 ## Think about it . . .

Consider each of the ways you can care for the spiritual temple of your body: hygiene, nutrition, movement, and rest. Which of these do you think you do a good job caring for? Why and how? Which of them do you think you could improve on? What's *one* change you could make this week that would honor God in the way you are caring for your body?

The Bible tells us our bodies are a temple of the Holy Spirit. How does thinking of your body as God's home change the way you treat it? Because the Holy Spirit lives within you, it would only make sense that he wants to help take care of his home—your body. What do you think this means, and how can you work *with* the Holy Spirit to maintain your body?

> Therefore, I urge you, brothers and sisters, in view of God's mercy, to offer your bodies as a living sacrifice, holy and pleasing to God—this is your true and proper worship.
>
> ROMANS 12:1

How does this verse connect to or support what you've learned about your body as a temple and how to care for it?

 ## Pray about it . . .

- Tell God the areas in which you struggle to care for your body well. Be specific about why this is hard for you.

- Thank him for providing you with this body.

- Ask him to help you treat your body well and maintain his physical home in a way that honors him.

Complaining Is Easier Than Complimenting

Relationships

Do not let any unwholesome talk come out of your mouths, but
only what is helpful for building others up according to their needs,
that it may benefit those who listen.

Ephesians 4:29

There is one thing I'll say about middle school girls—actually, I'll say it about females in general—they don't let each other complain alone. Do you know what I'm talking about? When someone criticizes herself, we immediately jump in with a complaint of our own. It's as if we don't want anyone feeling bad about themselves by themselves.

Here, let me show you. Listen in on this conversation in the locker room after gym class:

"I'm so fat. My stomach is just gross."

"Well, at least you can't play connect-the-dots on your face. It doesn't matter how much I wash it; it's still oily, filled with pimples, and disgusting."

"At least you don't look like a third grader. I'm so short, someone at the game the other day thought my little sister was older than me."

"My chest looks like it belongs to a third grader."

"You have good hair, though; mine's all nasty and stringy. I don't even know what to do with it."

I'm right, aren't I? You've been caught in the middle of a complaining conversation, haven't you?

I think those kinds of conversations break God's heart. He looks down on that locker room and sees a room full of beautiful girls, girls that he created uniquely and purposefully, bodies he intentionally designed to function for living, and all he hears are complaints.

Imagine if you spent hours painting, crafting, baking, drawing, writing . . . only to have people look at your work and criticize it. Kind of defeating, huh?

I don't think God feels defeated by your complaints, because he knows the truth about who you are and who he created you to be. He knows his work is good and doesn't need us to recognize it for it to be true. But I think it's time to shift our conversations to reflect God's glory (yes, I'm talking to myself too) because those conversations can lead to *us* feeling defeated about ourselves.

We usually think of unwholesome talk as *bad* words—those four-letter ones they bleep out in the *edited* versions of songs. But I think the negative conversations we have about ourselves (both internally and with others) are also examples of unwholesome talk. The original Greek word used in Ephesians 4:29 for *unwholesome* is *sapros* and is defined as "rotten, worthless."[1] That's exactly what these complaining conversations are . . . rotten.

Think about an apple left sitting in your locker—you might notice a little brown mushy spot, but it's easy enough to ignore and let sit. Each day you open your locker and ignore the apple, not realizing that the little rotten spot has grown bigger and bigger until, finally, one day you notice the smell. You reach for the apple and it squishes in your hand, icky, sticky juices dripping down your arm. You immediately drop it in the trash and begin to clean up the mess it left in your locker.

A complaint here and there, a critique of your own appearance after a friend critiques her own, is a small rotten spot. But when it's allowed to happen again and again, day after day, the rotten—unwholesome—talk spreads, and defeat and decay begin to spread through your heart.

How might these complaining conversations change if you took a big, bold step and met a friend's complaint with a compliment? Maybe something like this.

"I'm so fat. My stomach is gross."

"You're not gross. You have the best hair. And you are one of the nicest people I know."

What would follow? Girls chiming in with complaints about their own physical appearance? More rotten words? Maybe. But I doubt it. It might be met with a look of shock and a shrug of the shoulders before the conversation drifted to another topic. Or maybe your compliment might actually be followed by others—a conversation full of building each other up.

And that's the kind of conversation that is pleasing to God's ears.

❋ Think about it . . .

If you're going to make an effort to stop the group complaints (unwholesome talk) and shift the conversation to compliments, you need to prepare for the next opportunity. Think about the girls you spend the most time with, those with whom you might get caught up in a conversation of complaints, and list their names below. Next to each of their names, write one or two things you could compliment them on—don't limit yourself to compliments about their physical traits, but consider what you love about their personality too. This way you're ready to build them up the next time their own words are less than complimentary.

This week's verse in Ephesians tells us to build each other up, and you've already considered how you can encourage your friends by complimenting them. But what about those who aren't your friends? Might they need to be built up too? Maybe it's a girl you sit next to in math class but rarely talk to. Maybe it's the new kid who hasn't quite found his or her place with a group of friends yet. Maybe it's a sibling (they're not *always* annoying). Or maybe it's a parent or a teacher (adults need to be built up too).

List three to five people you could compliment who you might not normally build up. Write down some ideas about what you could compliment them about—make sure your words are true and sincere. Then, over the next several days (depending on how many people you list), commit to building others up with your compliments. When you're done, come back here and answer this question. What did giving compliments to others give back to you?

> **The words of the reckless pierce like swords, but the tongue of the wise brings healing.**
>
> PROVERBS 12:18

How does this verse connect to or support what you've learned about the effect of complaints and compliments?

 Pray about it . . .

- Thank God for putting people in your life who build you up; be specific and speak their names.

- Admit that you tend to complain more than compliment, and ask God to forgive you for being so quick to criticize yourself and get caught up in negative conversations.

- Ask God to give you opportunities this week to build others up and for the courage to speak boldly.

Why Does Shopping Have to Be So Hard?

Living

Therefore, as God's chosen people, holy and dearly loved, clothe yourselves with compassion, kindness, humility, gentleness and patience.

Colossians 3:12

She stood on the other side of the dressing room door, peeling off her T-shirt and shorts and pulling on the tight, spandex material of a swimsuit. We had been to too many stores, and the fun of shopping was beginning to fade. She needed a swimsuit for this in-between phase. We were lost in a sea of options that didn't fit or didn't feel right.

I watched her hold up the girls' suits, stretching the fabric, hoping it might fit. We moved to the junior section, where she immediately rejected the tops that revealed more than her sports bra. Her fingers pinched at the padding in the cups that she couldn't and didn't want to fill.

Defeat settled in my heart. I joked and painted a smile on my face all while begging God to protect my daughter from the damage this shopping trip could do.

Because shopping is hard, isn't it?

I don't remember the abrupt jump in styles from girl to teen when I was growing up. Seeing it through my daughter's eyes painted a clear picture of the battle for her self-confidence and the struggle to discover her own style.

I wish I could say we ended that shopping trip with the perfect suit and her self-confidence strengthened. But the truth is, I held her as we sat in the dressing room, and we both cried. I prayed aloud over her, asking God to remind her where her worth, value, and confidence come from. I thanked him for the precious time we were given to spend together, just the two of us. We left that dressing room without a swimsuit. We endured an attack on her self-image, the first in a very long battle.

Those dressing rooms . . . they are battlegrounds. Clothes that don't fit litter the floor like debris from an explosion. Each time you open the door in search of a different size or style, the attack begins again. Bullets whiz past in the form of negative thoughts about your body—some barely missing, others hitting straight in the heart. And there you stand, naked and exposed. Literally, as you face that dressing room mirror, but also emotionally and spiritually naked and exposed to the assaults of the devil. And he is relentless.

The devil's strategy for this battle is simple: lie. He will whisper lies to you about how your body—God's creation—isn't good. He will scream in your face the lies of comparison, making you believe that other girls don't face this dressing room battle, that everything looks good on them. He'll plant land mines in the racks of clothes, anticipating the moment you'll step on them and he can batter you with the shrapnel of negativity about which size you are.

You need to prepare for this battle. Our God is the God of the dressing room. He walks beside you through this very battle, standing at your side, ready to fight.

But how do you do it? How do you fight this battle of self-confidence as you shop for clothes that fit your personality and your body?

You clothe yourself.

That's right: "as God's chosen people, holy and dearly loved, [you] clothe yourselves with compassion, kindness, humility, gentleness and patience" (Colossians 3:12).

Have compassion for yourself, recognizing that shopping is hard and your struggle is real. Be kind and gentle to yourself. Imagine shopping with a friend and telling her how good she looks or what you like about the clothes she's trying on, and then treat yourself with that same attitude. Embrace humility, understanding that not everything you try on will look great, but leave room for admitting when something does feel good and fits well. And most of all, have patience—with yourself and with the process. Don't give up on finding something you like because the first thing you picked out doesn't fit right. Have patience as you search, and be willing to try on many options as you discover what feels good on your body and gives you confidence.

Shopping can be hard—it can feel like a battle—but with God's help, you can clothe yourself for that battle and walk away victorious, even if your cart is empty.

 **Think about it . . .**

How would you describe your style? What kinds of clothing do you feel most comfortable and confident wearing? Imagine that no matter what kind of outfit you put on (dress, shorts, tank top, leggings, dressy clothes, overalls, romper, etc.), it fit your body well. What would you wear? Feel free to sketch a picture of your style or maybe even print off a picture and glue it to this page.

Think about the last time you tried on clothes. Did it feel like a battle? If so, what were the attacks focused on? What was your biggest struggle? How could remembering this verse and what we learned this week act as weapons in that battle?

If it did *not* feel like a battle, why didn't it? What went well? What could you learn from that experience that you could remember the next time you try new clothes on?

> **She is clothed with strength and dignity . . .**
>
> **PROVERBS 31:25A**

How does this verse connect to or support what you've learned about shopping and the way you treat yourself while looking for clothes?

 Pray about it . . .

We're going to try something a little different this week. Instead of me listing out the prayer points for you, I want you to consider what you have read and learned and write a dressing room prayer. I've left the four main prayer point starters for you if you want to use them, but you don't have to. The idea is to tell God how you feel about shopping and your body image. Think about things to thank him for—it could be things you've learned this week, things you're thankful for when it comes to clothes and shopping, or something about your body you're thankful for. Admit any struggles you have concerning clothes and body image and ask him for specific help.

Write a prayer that you can use the next time you step onto the battlefield of the dressing room. Once you've written it here, consider taking a picture of it or writing it on a small note card or sticky note and keeping it in your purse or wallet or whatever you might take with you shopping. Cover yourself in prayer, and clothe yourself with compassion, kindness, humility, gentleness, and patience.

- Tell God
- Thank him
- Admit
- Ask God

I Just Want to Fit In

My first car was a Chevy Astro van. Yep. I was sixteen and driving a 1990-something maroon van with a sliding door on one side. (Go ahead and google it so that you can really get the picture.)

While my friend could open up the passenger side of her two-door black car and throw her bags and books in the back, I was left sliding open the side door of my family-sized van in the parking lot after practice. Oh, and I often had to fill the radiator with a pitcher of water from the restaurant where I worked before leaving town so it wouldn't overheat before I got home.

It ran (most of the time) and got me where I needed to go, but it definitely wasn't the kind of car my friends were driving. I guess that was my first major experience in being different, accepting that I wasn't always going to be able to have or do the same things as other people. It's a lesson God's still teaching me today, but I'm learning that different is sometimes best. I'm hoping you can find that truth somewhere in these next pages too.

Following Jesus Is Worth It

God

Yet what we suffer now is nothing compared to the glory he will reveal to us later.

Romans 8:18 NLT

I babysat all day—I played with the kids, I made them lunch, I dealt with their whining, I changed the baby's diapers—all for $20. It wasn't worth it.

I work so hard at practice—I stay after and shoot, I run in the off-season to stay in shape, I give *everything* I can—and still, I sit on the bench. It's not worth it.

I'm trying to get my math grade up—I did every problem on my review sheet, I asked for extra help, I even prayed about it—but I still got a bad grade on the test. It wasn't worth all that extra work.

I was nice to her—I offered to be her partner when hers was gone, I complimented her, I gave her my cookie at lunch (even though I really wanted it)—all to be ignored after school. It wasn't worth it.

Have you ever been in one of these *not worth it* situations? When it seems like no matter what you do, the outcome isn't worth the work and sacrifice it took to get there. And because of that past outcome, you decide to just quit trying in the future because it wasn't worth it anyway. Some things in life are like that, and you have to decide whether or not the cost is worth it.

Sometimes being a Christian is going to make you wonder if the cost is worth the outcome.

Those times when you choose to do the right thing instead of what everyone else is doing. Those times when you boldly stand against what everyone else accepts as normal. Those times when you say no to invitations because you know that even though they're your friends, you know what they'll be doing won't honor the Lord and you'll feel trapped. Those times when people will make fun of you because you're "too good" to do the bad thing they're doing.

In those situations, it might not feel like it, but the cost of following Jesus is always worth the outcome because Jesus is worth it.

Why is Jesus worth it? Because Jesus decided *you* are worth it.

Jesus—fully man and fully God—chose to give up his seat in heaven. To be born as a human and to walk the dirty roads of this earth . . . for you.

God punished his only Son with the full wrath you deserve. God couldn't just ignore sin—he couldn't just say forget about it—because then he wouldn't be a holy and just God. He had to punish someone for the wrongs you have done and continue to do. Jesus accepted the righteous anger of his own Father as he hung on the cross . . . for you.

Is racking up likes on a social media post more appealing than the love of Jesus?

Is having friends to hang out with more treasured than a personal relationship with your Savior?

Is escaping ridicule more valuable than Christ's sacrifice on the cross?

Is being popular more important than loving like Jesus?

Is avoiding conflict more worthwhile than standing up for the Truth of the Bible?

As a Christian, you might have to give some things up, you might face ridicule, you might have to say no, you might feel like an outsider . . . but Jesus is worth it.

So yes, you may suffer and life might be hard, but it doesn't compare to the glory that will be revealed. With Jesus, the outcome is always worth the cost.

 **Think about it . . .**

Can you think of any situations when you (maybe without even really thinking about it) decided that the cost of following Jesus wasn't worth the outcome? Write about one below. In that situation, did you think, *I'm going to choose fitting in, being liked, avoiding conflict, etc. over God*, or did it just kind of happen? If you could go back to that situation, would you change what you did? What would you say or do differently?

You know what's amazing about God? He doesn't offer a blanket of forgiveness that he just kind of throws over your sins *once*, covering the stuff you did wrong *before* you were saved. God's forgiveness is continual— Jesus died for the bad choices of yesterday, the mistakes of today, and the wrongs you'll do tomorrow. That's part of what makes him worth it. You can never mess up too much for God to love and forgive you. How does knowing that God continuously loves and forgives you impact the way you live your everyday life? Does it make you want to live a life that honors Jesus's death? How can you do that?

> He was despised and rejected by mankind, a man of suffering, and familiar with pain. Like one from whom people hide their faces he was despised, and we held him in low esteem.
>
> ISAIAH 53:3

*Note: Isaiah is prophesying (predicting) about the Messiah; therefore, we understand that "he" refers to Jesus. Reread the verse, replacing the pronoun "he" with the name *Jesus*.

How does this verse connect to or support what you've learned about following Jesus and making choices that honor God being worth it?

 Pray about it . . .

- Tell God that he is worth suffering for.

- Thank him for the gift of salvation and his love and forgiveness.

- Admit that you sometimes choose what's easy or acceptable to avoid doing what's right (be specific).

- Ask God for forgiveness for those times, and ask him to remind you that he is worth it; ask him for the strength to follow him no matter what.

Standing Out When You Really Want to Fit In

Self

> If the world hates you, keep in mind that it hated me [Jesus] first. If you belonged to the world, it would love you as its own. As it is, you do not belong to the world, but I have chosen you out of the world. That is why the world hates you.
>
> John 15:18–19

I have the power to tell my mom!" I shouted across the playground at a group of girls. I was in fifth grade, maybe sixth, and this group of friends had been mean to someone—I think it was my little brother. The details are all a little blurry now, but the feelings from that day still stir up emotions in my all-grown-up heart.

I remember being angry, so angry that I blurted the words out before I had really even thought about them. I just wanted the girls to stop, but I had no real power over them—I wasn't the "queen bee," as we used to say. I was just a girl who usually went along with whatever the other girls did because I didn't want to cause trouble or get made fun of. Until that day.

I remember storming away with tears stinging my eyes. I had done it. I had taken a stand and, at the same time, likely secured my place as the outcast. Embarrassment and fear mingled in my heart, and I wondered if it would be worth it.

I'd love to tell you that those girls had a change of heart and suddenly stopped doing whatever it was that I was going to tell my mom about, but that's not what happened. As a matter of fact, they made fun of me for my little attempt to stand up for what was right. Even after the emotions of that day blew over and we were all friends again, occasionally they'd bring back the memory. They threw my words—"I have the power"—back at me in a mocking voice long after they had left my mouth. That's why I remember them so distinctly to this day.

Looking back, I guess that was my first bitter taste of the fact that standing out and fitting in aren't compatible.

You are going to face those moments too (maybe you already have). Those moments when you're going to have to choose to either stand out or fit in.

And it's going to be hard. You're going to be made fun of. You're going to be misunderstood. You might lose friends. You might become the outcast of your group.

But here's the thing. As a Christian, you *should* do things differently than those who aren't. People should look at you and say, "That girl is different from the rest."

Because you don't belong to the "world."

You don't belong to the popular group—they don't own you.

You don't belong to the do-whatever-feels-good culture.

You don't belong to the do-whatever-it-takes-to-fit-in mentality.

You. Belong. To. Jesus.

And the "world" hated him too.

He didn't belong to the popular group; in fact, they (the Pharisees) plotted to kill him.

He didn't belong to the do-whatever-feels-good culture; instead, he told people to turn from their sins.

He didn't belong to the do-whatever-it-takes-to-fit-in mentality; rather, he invited the outcasts to sit with him.

So when you taste the bitterness of standing out instead of fitting in, remember who stands beside you and taste the sweetness of his love.

He knows how it feels to do what's right and be treated wrong. You are not alone, even when it feels like you are. Jesus has been there and done that, and he is here now as you're doing this. He will give you strength. He will bring you comfort. And he will love you no matter what.

✳ Think about it . . .

Have you ever been in a lazy river at a waterpark? They're my favorite. I love sitting on a tube, drifting along without having to put forth any real effort, just floating where the current takes me. But sometimes lazy rivers have those little overhead waterfalls you're forced to go under—I hate those. I will do *anything* to avoid them. I'll paddle around them with my arms flailing. I'll get out of my tube and squeeze into the narrow space between the waterfall and the wall. I'll even walk against the current to climb up the steps and out of the river if I have to.

How does your life compare to a lazy river? In what ways do you just go with the flow? What kinds of waterfalls might the current be leading you toward that you know you should try to avoid? What might you have to do to escape them?

Think about a time when you had to make a choice to either stand out or fit in. Tell a little about the situation below and explain what you chose to do. What were the consequences of or reactions to your choice? What do you think Jesus would say to you about that situation if he were sitting next to you right now?

> **Jesus, our high priest, is able to understand our weaknesses. When Jesus lived on earth, he was tempted in every way. He was tempted in the same ways we are tempted, but he never sinned.**
>
> **HEBREWS 4:15 ERV**

How does this verse connect to or support what you've learned about choosing to stand out even when you really want to fit in?

 # Pray about it . . .

- Tell God that it is hard to fight the current and stand up for what is right; share specific examples you're facing right now.

- Thank Jesus for understanding how hard it is to stand out when you really want to fit in.

- Admit that it's easier to go with the flow and sometimes you've chosen that instead of standing up for what God thinks is right.

- Ask God to forgive you for those times, and ask him to give you the courage needed to stand out, even if it means not fitting in.

Is It Okay to Have Non-Christian Friends?

Relationships

Do not be misled: "Bad company corrupts good character."

1 Corinthians 15:33

During my early years of high school, I dealt with migraines—bad ones. When one would hit, I'd find myself unable to function. Light bothered me, noise hurt my head, and the pain was so bad I felt like I was going to throw up. My mom took me to the doctor in hopes of finding a medication that would ease the intensity of the migraines. Along with a prescription, I remember the doctor mentioning possible triggers, including dill pickles and chocolate—two foods I loved (not together, of course, that would be gross).

So I had a choice to make: continue eating them and risk triggering a migraine or avoid them and risk missing out on deliciousness. I chose and still choose a third option: be aware of the risks and eat them in moderation.

I think our approach to non-Christian friendships can be handled in a similar way. We don't have to completely avoid anyone who doesn't believe in Jesus, but we do need to be aware of the risks—the influence and effect they have on us.

So how should you choose your friends? And how do you know if it's okay to be friends with someone who doesn't share your Christian beliefs?

The answer is simple: do what Jesus did.

Before choosing his disciples, "Jesus went out to a mountainside to pray, and spent the night praying to God. When morning came, he called his disciples to him and chose twelve of them, whom he also designated apostles" (Luke 6:12–13). Before Jesus chose his closest friends and let them into his heart as the ones he trusted, he prayed.

That's where you start. You pray and ask God for guidance when choosing friends. You pray about your current friendships and ask God to show you any that don't honor him. You trust that God knows your heart *and theirs* and that he will lead you toward good friendships and away from dangerous ones.

So does that mean all your friends must be Christians? That if they can't mark off the boxes on some Christian-friend checklist, it's time to walk away? Not at all. Again, do what Jesus did.

In Mark 2, we find Jesus having dinner at Levi's house, and "many tax collectors and sinners were eating with him" (v. 15). As you read through the New Testament, you'll often find him with those we'd consider non-Christians.

Jesus spent time with people who *made* poor choices, but he was never influenced by them to *make* poor choices.

Evaluating friendships isn't about the friends—the people you hang out with—it's about the effect they have on you. Are they leading you into poor decision-making? Do you feel trapped when you're with them, as if you have no choice but to follow in behaviors that don't honor God? Do you find yourself becoming more like *them* and less like *Jesus*?

If you've answered yes to these questions, then it's likely time to take a step back from that friendship. That doesn't mean you have to give them the silent treatment or turn your back on them completely. You need to take time to pray about that friendship and ask God for guidance. It might mean continuing to be kind and offering friendship at school but not hanging out with them in other situations where you risk making poor choices. It might mean asking God for the courage to confront those friends about their choices, even if it risks your friendship. And it might mean completely walking away from the friendship because the effects of it are not healthy for you.

God commands us to love one another and to be a light for him. Relationships with non-Christian friends can be a chance for you to be a light. You can show love for an unbelieving friend by praying for him or her, sharing the story of God's love with them, or simply just treating them well. You can use friendships with nonbelievers to let your light shine, but you shouldn't let those relationships trap you into making poor decisions.

 Think about it . . .

What is your favorite thing to do with your friends? Describe the perfect girls' day out.

There are more than eight billion people in the world—and no two are exactly alike. Why might it be important to have friends who are different from you? How can your differences be a positive part of your friendship? Share any specific examples of why differences are important in your friendships.

> **Don't befriend angry people or associate with hot-tempered people, or you will learn to be like them and endanger your soul.**
>
> PROVERBS 22:24–25 NLT

How does this verse connect to or support what you've learned about friendships?

 Pray about it . . .

- Tell God how awesome it is that he has created billions of people and yet none of them have ever been exactly alike.

- Thank him for your friendships.

- Ask him for guidance in choosing your friends and to show you if there are any friendships that have a negative influence on you.

- Admit any fears or worries you have about friendship and ask him to give you what you need in those situations.

Do I Really Have to Be Different?

Living

> Don't copy the behavior and customs of this world, but let God transform you into a new person by changing the way you think. Then you will learn to know God's will for you, which is good and pleasing and perfect.
>
> Romans 12:2 NLT

There's an old, popular Sunday school song about telling our eyes to be careful what they see and our ears to be careful what they hear. Do you know which one I'm talking about?

It has a catchy tune that makes it easy to remember, and though it may seem rather childish, it actually has a powerful message behind it. God is looking down on us and sees inside our hearts. Everything we see and hear influences our thoughts, which God also sees.

Turn on the television. How many shows can you find free of cuss words, inappropriate behavior, or negative messages? Open up your music streaming app. How many songs do you hear that are free of inappropriate lyrics or negative messages (even the edited versions)? If you watch and listen closely, the answer to both questions is likely very few.

Unfortunately, the world in which we live is full of negative messages. Many people think you can watch shows and listen to songs that contain messages contrary to God's will without being affected. I used to. I remember trying to defend listening to Eminem, a popular rapper in the early 2000s: "I know the lyrics are inappropriate, I just like the beat and sound of the music." And I did the same with what I watched: "Yeah, sometimes the characters on that show treat others poorly, but I know better. I can watch that show that portrays characters doing bad things—I know it's wrong, and I'd never do that."

Sound at all familiar? But the truth is, everything you allow your eyes to see and your ears to hear influences your thoughts and actions.

After watching your favorite show in which the main character is rude and disrespectful to her parents, you may catch yourself telling your mom to just leave you alone when she asks how your day was. You may begin humming that catchy tune you heard on the radio, and before you know it, you're singing along to the words—words you wouldn't normally say aloud.

Remember how your body is a temple of the Holy Spirit? Our spiritual temples don't necessarily have bricks for walls; it's more like the screen on a storm door. As you listen and watch, words and messages enter the temple of your mind through the screen. Once inside, they hang out for a while, maybe get stuck in a corner (lyrics you can't get out of your head), but eventually, they find their way out again.

Those negative words and messages come in through the screen and then flow right back out through your behavior. Sometimes without you even realizing it.

Even though you don't think shows and music influence you, they begin seeping into your actions. For this reason, we must be careful of what we see and hear. We must be careful of what we allow to flow through the screen-walls of our temple of heart, soul, and mind.

Guarding your temple might make you look different to the outside world. You might get strange looks when you admit you haven't heard that song or you don't watch that series. People might think you're weird because you're not on that social media app. And you might feel a little excluded.

But protecting your temple is more important than what anyone else thinks or says about you.

PS: This might be why your parents are so strict about technology. It's not because they don't *get it*. It's because they know the dangers out there (far scarier than bad lyrics and negative messages), and they're trying to protect you from them. Try to give them some grace. They're doing their best. And they love you. A lot.

✳ Think about it . . .

Make a list of three of your favorite songs. Look up the lyrics to them and read them word for word. Do they contain any words you would be ashamed to say in front of your parents? Would you sing them in front of Jesus? Do they contain a message about relationships between men and women? What is that message? Do you agree with it? Would your parents? Would Jesus?

Consider your mind to be the center of your temple, kind of like the living room where the Holy Spirit hangs out. It's like he's standing at the door with his hand on the knob—together, you can decide what to let in and what to keep out. Are the things coming through it things the Holy Spirit would happily open the door to? Is there anything you've been letting in that the Holy Spirit might want you to shut the door on?

Instead of an extra verse to look at this week, I want you to explore Christian music. People often limit Christian music to songs sung in church. However, there is a whole world of Christian artists who offer different styles of music such as contemporary, rap, pop, dance, and many more. It is not limited to church music.

Go to Google or YouTube or Spotify and search for "Christian music," then scroll through and listen to a few songs until you find one you like. Throughout this week, try to find at least one new song a day. Keep track of the artists and songs you like below.

Pray about it . . .

- Tell God that it is hard to be different, that you don't like feeling like you're the only one who doesn't . . . (watch that show, listen to that music, have a phone, get on Snapchat, etc.).

- Ask God to help provide music and entertainment that is worthy of entering your temple and to help you make good choices about what you see and hear.

- Thank him for Christian artists who provide an alternative, at least in the music industry, and ask him to give them the strength and courage to continue to produce music that honors him.

- Ask God to give *you* the strength and courage to keep things out of your temple that don't honor him and to accept the impact it might have on what people think of you.

I'm Just a Kid

Sometimes it can feel like you're just floating in a river of changing currents with childhood along one bank and teenage life on the other. You're just waiting for the current to push you to one bank or the other, like you have no purpose in this in-between season. You're outgrowing the carefree days of childhood, but you're not quite sure you want to step onto the bank of becoming a teen and all the responsibility that comes with it.

But there is purpose in this in-between. It's a place where God uses the current to wash away old things and uncover new. It's a confusing, hard, and (believe it or not) beautiful place to be. This in-between space is where God begins to shape you. It's the space where he guides your heart from one bank to the other, out of the comfort of childhood faith and into the boldness of your own.

I'm praying for you with each of these devotions, asking God to help you discover the relationship he made you to have with him.

I'm Pretty Sure God Doesn't Want to Use Me

God

> The LORD said to him, "Who gave human beings their mouths? Who makes them deaf or mute? Who gives them sight or makes them blind? Is it not I, the LORD? Now go; I will help you speak and will teach you what to say."
>
> Exodus 4:11–12

Do you know Moses? (No, not the cute boy who sits two rows in front of you in class . . . the Moses from the Bible.) The baby placed in a basket found by Pharaoh's daughter. The kid who was raised in a palace. The guy who warned Pharaoh about the plagues (locusts, frogs, flies, oh my!). The one who led his people out of slavery and held his hands up as the waters of the Red Sea parted so the Israelites could walk across on dry ground. You know, *that* Moses.

Maybe you knew all that or maybe you didn't. Either way, you know now, and you might think Moses was the perfect guy for the job. The kind of guy who gets picked first for everything—smart, fine, talented, smooth, *and* nice. The guy all the girls want to date and the guys want to be.

And while it's true that God used him in amazing ways, you need to know the whole story to really know Moses. You see, Moses *killed* a guy.

He was walking around the city and saw an Egyptian beating a Hebrew; Moses got angry, beat the Egyptian, and hid the body in the sand. Then he ran away. For forty years he lived an uneventful life in the land of Midian.

Then one day he noticed a bush in flames, yet not burning away. He went to investigate, and there he met God's presence. God told him that he would be the one to lead the Hebrews out of Egypt. But Moses wasn't a fan of that plan. He argued that no one would believe that God had chosen him. He argued that no one would listen to him. He argued that he wasn't a good enough speaker to stand up to Pharaoh and lead a nation. He even begged God to send someone else.

But you know what God said? I don't care. I created you. I know you. And besides, this isn't about you . . . it's about *me* and what I can do *through* you.

So Moses (a little reluctantly) went and did as God said. He became the Moses you know today.

I think God has a similar message for you. He created you. He knows you. And he wants to work through you. Not because you're perfect and full of awesomeness, but because he is perfect and full of more power than you can even imagine.

The same God who used Moses to send plagues to Egypt and part the Red Sea wants to use *you*. It doesn't matter how unworthy or incapable you feel because it's not about you. It's about God's power and might. It's about God's goodness. It's about how great he is.

We forget about that sometimes, don't we? We forget how great God is. We forget that it was *his* power that parted the Red Sea (Exodus 14). It was *his* power that sent manna into the wilderness (Exodus 16). It was *his* power that made the sun and moon stand still (Joshua 10). It was *his* power that kept Daniel safe in the lions' den (Daniel 6). God worked through people, but the power was *his*.

His power can work through you too. You just have to be willing. You have to be like Moses. Because even though he doubted and feared, he still *went*. He left Midian and went to Egypt, trusting that God's power was enough. And *his* power is enough for you too.

 Think about it . . .

Write down three words to describe Moses *before* he returned to Egypt to rescue his people. In what ways can you relate to those?

God probably isn't going to ask you to lead a nation out of captivity or part a sea, but that doesn't mean he can't use you. Take a minute to ask God how he might want to use you right now. Pray, and then sit quietly and let him guide your thoughts. Write down what he leads you to think about—little ways he might want to use you right now. Over the next few days, be looking for ways to serve him in your daily life.

> **Finally, be strong in the Lord and in his mighty power.**
>
> EPHESIANS 6:10

How does this verse connect to or support what you've learned about your ability to be used by God?

 Pray about it ...

- Tell God how awesome he is and the ways you've seen his power at work. (Think about the work he did through Moses and examples from your life.)

- Thank him that he uses imperfect, incapable people to do his work.

- Admit your doubts and fears to God—explain how you feel about the possibility of him wanting to use you.

- Ask God to help you focus on *his* power and not your weakness. Ask him to show you little ways he can use you this week and to give you the courage to follow through.

Why Try?

Now to him who is able to do immeasurably more than all we ask or imagine, according to his power that is at work within us, to him be glory in the church and in Christ Jesus throughout all generations, for ever and ever! Amen.

Ephesians 3:20–21

Draw me a hippo." Her big brown eyes looked up at me as she handed me the chalk.

No was on my lips, but before it could spill out, she asked again.

"Draw me a hippo," she insisted.

I *almost* said, "*Mommy can't draw*," but she didn't know I couldn't. She thought I could draw her a hippo, a giraffe, a lion, or the Mona Lisa. My two-year-old had the unshakable confidence that I could do *anything*—even draw a hippo with sidewalk chalk.

My confidence in my abilities? Not so much.

When does that happen? When do we lose that confidence? When do we transition from *anything is possible* to *there's no way I can do that*?

Has it happened to you? Are you already there? Have you shed the skin that believes you can at least *try* new things and instead grown the thick armor of *if I don't try, I don't have to face the possibility of failure*?

Because that's what happens, isn't it? We learn what failure feels like and decide that not trying is the better option. And so, we stop trying. We stop believing that we're able to do anything. And maybe we even start to think we are capable of nothing.

That day with my daughter, I got out my phone, googled cartoon images of a hippo, and picked up the chalk. My drawing wasn't perfect. It *sort of* looked like the image I was trying to copy. But I did it. I tried.

And I think in that moment, God was trying to teach me something I wish I had learned many years ago . . . it's okay to try. It's okay to try new things and see if God might be leading you to something you never would have imagined you'd like and never would have dreamed you were good at.

The point here isn't to have confidence in yourself, it's to have confidence in your God. God created you and has seen every moment of your future. You never know how your actions today will impact tomorrow, but he does.

In 2007, I participated in a grammar workshop (I loved every second of it, and now you know I'm a complete nerd). I was a new teacher learning about a new program to teach grammar to middle school students. I didn't have a strong background in grammar, was about as clueless as the kids in my classroom, and knew I needed to find a better way to teach kids where to put commas, so I went to this workshop. I tried something new.

Fast-forward to forty-year-old me. I have a part-time job editing content for a website that publishes hundreds of articles each year and has over a million followers.

I could not do this job had I not tried something new over fifteen years ago. God used that grammar workshop to lead me toward a career in writing.

Could it be that God is leading you toward something right now that will impact you decades later? Maybe it's leading to a career. Maybe it's leading to a lifelong hobby. Maybe it's leading you to friendships he doesn't want you to live without.

I don't want you to miss out on beautiful things tomorrow because you're too afraid to try today.

So just do it. Pick up the chalk and draw the hippo. Let God do the rest. He is, after all, "able to do immeasurably more than all we ask or imagine" (Ephesians 3:20).

 Think about it . . .

What is the last new thing you've tried? (This doesn't have to be some big thing—an activity, a new food, a new class, a different kind of book, etc.) Why did you try it? Did you like it? Why or why not?

What opportunities are there for you to try new things right now? (After-school clubs, sports, or activities. Classes you could sign up for. Things to do with friends. Something you've thought about trying before but never have.) What keeps you from trying those new things? Choose one new thing that you're most willing to try. What's the worst thing that could happen as a result of trying it? What's the best thing?

> "For I know the plans I have for you"—this is the LORD's declaration—"plans for your well-being, not for disaster, to give you a future and a hope."
>
> JEREMIAH 29:11 CSB

How does this verse connect to or support what you've learned about trying new things?

 Pray about it . . .

- Tell God about the things you want to try.

- Ask him to show you if there is anything *he* wants you to try.

- Thank him for knowing your future and leading you to things today that will impact your tomorrow.

- Admit that you need him to lead you because you are just a human who can't see what the future holds.

- Ask him to help you be brave and courageous to try new things.

I'm Not an Influencer

Relationships

> Don't let anyone look down on you because you are young, but
> set an example for the believers in speech, in conduct, in love, in
> faith and in purity.
>
> 1 Timothy 4:12

My sixteen-year-old daughter can drive herself to Claire's over an hour away. She can use her debit card funded with money from her after-school job and buy earrings. But she cannot get her ears pierced without my signature. She's too young.

You've likely been told that too. You're too young to drive, too young to get a job, too young to have a boyfriend (okay, I might agree with that one, but we'll talk about that later), too young to watch that movie, too young to go there by yourself, too young to have a phone, too young to do just about anything you want to do.

Right?

You want to know something you're not too young for? To be an influencer.

Wait, wait, wait. I don't mean *that* kind of influencer. The ones on social media telling you to buy this makeup or wear that outfit. The ones who determine what's in and what's out.

I'm talking about real influence in real life. And you have the ability to do that right now. You have the ability to influence younger brothers and sisters, kids you babysit for, your friends (your not-friends), and even adults around you. Your influence is powerful.

It's so easy to believe that God can't use you—especially right now in these in-between years—or that you have no influence. You're just a kid, after all.

But that's not how God sees you. God sees you as his handiwork, created in Christ Jesus to do the work he's already planned for you (see Ephesians 2:10). You are the perfect age to be an influencer for the Lord. At *every* age he wants you to follow the example he has set. Not only that, but he wants you to lead others by that example.

Let's go back—way back—to the 60s. Not the 1960s . . . the *sixties*, like AD 62–64, the first century after Christ's birth, death, and resurrection.

Timothy was a young pastor at the church in Ephesus, and he was struggling with challenges, conflict, and pressure, partly because he was a young man trying to lead believers and a church. Scholars believe he was not quite forty. Now, I know that sounds old to you, but considering the time period and his position as a leader, it was quite young. And his role as a follower of Christ and a leader began much earlier. Timothy accompanied Paul on a missionary journey years before, likely when Timothy was in his late teens or early twenties.

Now you know a little about Timothy, but what you really need to know is that Paul (and God) recognized his ability to influence others, no matter how many years old he was.

The book of First Timothy is Paul's letter of encouragement to his friend and fellow Christian. Paul tells him not to let anyone look down on him because he is young (1 Timothy 4:12). Paul's advice stretches across the gap of time and space to reach you today. These same words apply to you.

No matter your age or how old you are in your relationship with Christ as your personal Savior, God calls on you to set an example for others. He wants you to be an influencer.

This doesn't mean you need to start up an Instagram or TikTok account and share Bible verses every day. It simply means that in your real-life world, you live for Jesus. You show kindness to the new kid. You step away from those who are doing wrong. You invite the overlooked to sit with you at lunch. You follow directions and listen in class (even if your classmates aren't). You take pride in your work—in the classroom, on the court or field or diamond, and at home—because you want to honor God in the work you do. You choose words that build up and encourage rather than tear down.

You become an influencer for Christ when you live your daily life in a way that shows Jesus is walking beside you. And, trust me, you're not too young for that.

 Think about it . . .

Name someone older than you who has influenced you. How has that person impacted you? What do you do differently because of the example he or she has set?

Among people your age, name someone who has influenced you. How has that person impacted you? What do you do differently because of the example he or she has set? (PS: Influence isn't always positive, so if there is someone who has made a negative impact, it's okay to write about that too.)

> **For we are God's handiwork, created in Christ Jesus to do good works, which God prepared in advance for us to do.**
>
> **EPHESIANS 2:10**

How does this verse connect to or support what you've learned about your ability to be an influencer?

 Pray about it . . .

- Thank God for being an influence in your life and for giving you the Bible so that you can know how to live for him.

- Admit that you are not always a positive influencer, and tell him about specific times when you've either been a poor influence or have missed the chance to be a good one and ask him to forgive you.

- Ask God to make you aware of the influence you have and to give you opportunities to make an impact.

- Ask him to help you be bold and courageous for him.

All Work Is Worthy

Living

Trust in the LORD with all your heart; do not depend on your own understanding. Seek his will in all you do, and he will show you which path to take.

Proverbs 3:5–6 NLT

My dad is a farmer. When he graduated from high school, he worked for the local coop and continued to work on his family's dairy. After my grandpa died, my dad and one of my uncles continued working the dairy. My dad woke up early in the morning to milk cows before coming home to help us get ready for school. He spent his days making sure his Holsteins had everything they needed. He planted, cultivated, and harvested in order to store up enough grain to feed them all year long. He baled hay and put up fences. He hauled manure (that's a *polite* word for poop) and washed out the milking stalls. My dad worked hard.

Most of my friends' dads were farmers, too, or their jobs were in some way related to agriculture. It never really occurred to me that my dad was *just* a farmer. But then I went to college, and I met people whose dads were businessmen or doctors or lawyers. Being from a farm felt like a downgraded life compared to others. My dad's job title of farmer didn't seem as impressive as others.

But my dad . . . he was made to farm. His problem-solving skills are among the best I have ever seen. When a piece of equipment breaks down, he digs through the shed for spare parts and washers and bolts or whatever else he might need, and he figures it out. He fixes it. He knows what to feed the livestock and when. He can deliver a baby calf and knows what to do when it gets sick. My dad doesn't have multiple degrees or a lot of zeros in his paycheck, but he does the work God created him to do.

This world teaches us that value comes from our job titles. That the doctor is more valuable than the welder. Or the CEO more important than the person in the factory assembling products. But the reality is that *all* work is worthy when it's done for the Lord.

If you want to be *important* in this world, do the work God has created you to do. Your future path is about your heart. It's about having a heart that recognizes who made you. It's about a heart that desires to do what God asks more than what the world says is valuable. It's about a heart that follows God's lead even when it's hard or scary or unconventional. It's about a heart that trusts his plan more than your own.

I want you to discover the path God has laid out for you, and I want you to run down it. I don't care if it comes with a small paycheck. I don't care if it means you come home dirty and exhausted. I don't care if you wear a skirt and heels or scrubs and tennis shoes. I want you to do the work God has created you for, and I want you to do it well.

And I pray that when you discover that path and do that work, that you will never let anyone make you feel like *just a* _____. I pray that you will see great value in the work God created you to do. I pray that you chase his purpose for you rather than frantically try to climb a ladder for a *better* job title. God's path is full of purpose, and you're the perfect one to walk it.

 # Think about it . . .

Make a list of the jobs the adults in your family have (your parents, grandparents, aunts, uncles, or any other important adults in your life). We've been talking about how it's hard feeling like you're just a kid and wondering how God can use you. Do you think any of the adults in your list sometimes question the value of their jobs? Might they think, *I'm just a ____?* Circle any of those jobs that other people might consider unimportant.

Look at the list you made above. Choose two of those jobs and explain why they are important and how God might be using those people through their jobs.

> **Yet you, LORD, are our Father. We are the clay, you are the potter; we are all the work of your hand.**
>
> **ISAIAH 64:8**

How does this verse connect to or support what you've learned about the value of doing the work God created you for?

 # Pray about it . . .

- Admit that sometimes you fail to recognize the importance of some jobs and consider them to be less valuable.

- Thank God for the people who do those jobs and ask him to help them feel valued and appreciated.

- Thank him for being such a personal God that he would make specific plans just for you, and ask him to make your path clear for the future and to give you courage to do what he created you for and to take pride in that work.

Is Sin Even Important?

Sin. It's kind of a harsh word. It sounds so, well, judgy. In fact, outside church, you probably never use the word. No one really talks about sin.

But just because we don't say the word doesn't mean it doesn't exist. Sometimes it gets disguised as *poor choices*, *wrong decisions*, or even *mistakes*. The Bible is clear, though: if you're a human, you're also a sinner. But thank God, we don't have to stay stuck in that sin because he offers grace and forgiveness. Over the next few weeks, we're going to talk about all this.

God Is Holy.
Why Does It Matter?

God

> There is no one holy like the LORD; there is no one besides you; there is no Rock like our God.
>
> 1 Samuel 2:2

Goody-two-shoes, brown-noser, teacher's pet, Miss Perfect—I've been called them all. And I claimed a few of those titles with pride.

I remember being a little confused the first time someone uttered such insults at me. Why was it such a bad thing to be good? To follow the rules? To do what you were told? There I was, doing what was right and being told that it was wrong—and definitely not popular. (This may shock you, but I went to a small church school, and even there it wasn't always *cool* to be good.)

Goody-two-shoes . . . of course I was—I didn't want to cause trouble, and disappointing people was on my list of don't ever dos.

Brown-noser, teacher's pet . . . well, if by that you mean work hard and do everything within your means to be a good student and get good grades, then, yes, that was me.

Miss Perfect . . . boy, did I chase perfection.

And though I admit to being many of these things, despite my best efforts, I could never actually be perfect. No matter how hard I worked to please others, obey my parents, listen to my teachers, and do what was right—no matter how hard I tried to look *perfect* on the outside—the truth is, I was far from perfect and nowhere near holy.

That's kind of hard to admit, even today. If you could have peeked behind that curtain of perfection or holiness that I put up for others to see, you would have seen a middle school girl with a bad attitude, a heart often spiked with anger, and a whole lot of feeling not good enough.

Maybe you can relate. Maybe you're a good-on-the-outside kind of girl who hates what she sees behind the curtain. Or maybe you're the one who only sees the curtain, who pokes fun at *Miss Perfect* but deep down inside wonders why it's so easy for her to be good and for you to be awful.

Here's the thing: you two are the same. The *good* girl and the *bad* girl are really both just girls—born sinful, in need of grace, and far from perfect.

I know it's not fun to think about that. It's not encouraging to think about how sinful we are or to recognize all the bad things we've done and continue to do. But I think it's necessary. Because when we look at ourselves and see our sin, we also see our need for our Savior. We discover that we are unholy humans, wholly loved by a holy God.

Holiness is only found in God, a life of perfection only in Jesus. No matter how *good* you (or other people, even adults) look, you cannot live up to God's standards. Righteousness is *who* God is, not just how he acts. God defines holiness because he *is* holy. Jesus lived a perfect, sinless life because he *was* perfect.

So what do we do with this?

Do we say . . . *Well, fine, God, you are holy, and I never can be, so I may as well give up. It's not possible. Why even try to do what's right?*

I mean, you could, but I'm afraid that path is littered with disappointment, failure, and a sense of feeling lost and unloved.

Instead, maybe say this . . . *God, you are holy, and that is amazing. I can't be perfect for a day—or even an hour—but, Lord, you are holy and perfect and righteous. You don't even have to try. You set the standard for holiness. And, God, I know I can't live up to that standard no matter how hard I try. But I love you and I trust you and I want to be more like you. Can you show me how? Can you help me see your holiness and chase after it, not because I think I can be good enough for you, but because I think you can be the good in me?*

Instead of pursuing perfection, chase after becoming like Christ—through his power in you.

Instead of hiding from your unholiness, stand in awe of who God is and his holiness.

Instead of working to please people, let the Holy Spirit work in your heart.

God's holiness shouldn't intimidate you and make you feel worthless; it should inspire you to worship him and be in awe of his love for you—the love of a holy God who loves you even in your unholiness. We'll talk more about that love next week, but for now, can you accept your imperfections and recognize your sin so that you can see God's holiness more clearly?

Think about it . . .

What do people see when they look at you? What would they see if they peeked behind the curtain?

What is one thing you've done in the last twenty-four hours that you think Jesus would have done differently? How does looking at your imperfection help you appreciate the perfection of Jesus more?

God's holiness can be confusing . . . I still have questions too. Use the link to watch this video from Bible Project, and then answer the questions below: BibleProject.com/explore/video/holiness/

How did the video help you understand God's holiness and our imperfections?

How does Jesus connect us (unholy people) to our holy God?

 Pray about it . . .

- Tell God how much you admire his holiness, his perfection.

- Admit that you cannot be holy and that you are far from perfect.

- Ask God to help you not to be discouraged by his holiness and your imperfection but instead to be in awe of it, and ask him for help to understand it.

- Thank God for sending Jesus so that we no longer have to be separated from God's holiness but can be made pure through his sacrificial death.

Life Isn't Fair but God Is

Self

> We are made right with God by placing our faith in Jesus Christ. And this is true for everyone who believes, no matter who we are. For everyone has sinned; we all fall short of God's glorious standard. Yet God, in his grace, freely makes us right in his sight. He did this through Christ Jesus when he freed us from the penalty for our sins.
>
> Romans 3:22–24 NLT

It's not fair. Why do I get my phone taken away for yelling at him, but he can call me names and tell me I'm worthless, and he doesn't even get in trouble?

I did *all* the work for this group project. No one even tried to help me; they just messed around on their iPads while I did everything and even brought it home to finish. They did nothing, but they get the same grade as me. How is that fair?

My friends get to go to the movies by themselves, they get to walk around town on their own after practice, and their parents don't hover around them like they're little babies. It's not fair that I got stuck with such overprotective parents.

I want you to think about the words *fairness* and *justice*. Because I think you're right—there are situations in life that just aren't fair—and I think it's important for you to recognize them.

I googled the words *fairness* and *justice* and put together these definitions based on what I found:

Fairness: impartial and just treatment or behavior without favoritism or discrimination

Justice: treatment according to what is just (what is morally right and fair)

So, if your younger brother or sister gets something that you didn't get at that same age, that would be unfair. There seems to be favoritism. If you get punished for something you've done wrong, that would be justice, but if someone else doesn't get punished for similar behavior, it would be unjust. Right?

Now, let's think of this in terms of God. Remember how we talked last week about how holy God is? He doesn't just *act* righteous (without flaw), he *is* righteous.

If God is holy, that also means he is fair and just. In fact, the Bible tells us, "He is the Rock; his deeds are perfect. Everything he does is just and fair. He is a faithful God who does no wrong; how just and upright he is!" (Deuteronomy 32:4 NLT).

If we believe God is just, then we understand that he has to treat sin with justice—meaning that those who sin must be punished for that sin.

If we believe God is fair, then we understand that in his fairness he must punish *all* who sin—no one gets a pass—meaning that each of us deserves punishment, "For everyone has sinned; we all fall short of God's glorious standard" (Romans 3:23 NLT).

Are you following me? If God is fair and just, he *has* to punish sin. And if we are born sinful, *we* deserve that punishment. That would be fair and just.

Now think about Jesus. He never sinned, not once. Not even that time his brother made him *really* mad (yes, he had siblings, and yes, I'm sure they were annoying). Jesus lived a perfect life, so according to our sense of fairness and justice, he didn't deserve to be punished.

But listen to this . . .

Because God is fair and just, because he is holy and *hates* sin, he had to do something about all these sinners running around the world. He couldn't just let their sins go unpunished—that wouldn't be fair, that wouldn't bring justice. He *had* to punish them; it's who he is. Don't worry, though, God had a plan from the moment Eve took a bite of that fruit.

Jesus was his plan. And Jesus was a willing part of that plan.

You see, sin needed to be punished, so Jesus stepped in and took our place. Jesus hung on the cross where you should have been, where I should have hung. Fairness and justice say that sin must be punished. And because you and I are sinners, that punishment belongs to us.

But God doesn't ask us to go to the cross because Jesus already did. The nails went through *his* hands, *his* feet. He hung on the cross, feeling forsaken by his Father, as all of God's righteous anger poured out. He suffered for your sin, for my sin. That doesn't seem fair, does it?

What an awesome God. A God who is fair and just *and* loving.

What an awesome Savior. A Savior who understands fairness and justice *and* loves you and me enough to die with our sins on his shoulders.

What an awesome story. One that didn't end on that cross or even in the tomb where Jesus's body was laid. Because the resurrection was also a part of the plan. Jesus rose from the dead, showing the almighty power of God.

Jesus's death reveals the fairness and justice of God's character because he couldn't let sin go unpunished.

Jesus's resurrection reveals God's love, redemption, and perfect plan because our sins have been paid for in a way we could *never* afford.

So what do we do with that? We accept the free gift of grace. We hold on to it as a reminder of what fairness, justice, and love mean. We open it up again and again, every time we mess up and ask for forgiveness. And we live to share it with others, telling them that life isn't fair or just, but God is, and he loves them more than they could ever imagine.

 ## Think about it . . .

Can you add your own examples of ways that life doesn't feel fair? What might God be trying to teach you through these things?

What questions do you have about God's righteousness, fairness, and justice? What confuses you about salvation? Write them below.

Did you know it's okay to have questions? I wish I could sit down beside you right now and open my Bible and look for answers together, but I don't have a hologram version of me yet. Instead, maybe you can take your questions to a youth group leader, your pastor, your parents, a friend's mom, or someone else who can help you understand the Bible more. Write your questions down and the name of someone who can help you dig for the answers. (PS: You can find me at LovingOurLord.com if you want to send them to me.)

> **For God chose to save us through our Lord Jesus Christ, not to pour out his anger on us. Christ died for us so that, whether we are dead or alive when he returns, we can live with him forever.**
>
> **1 THESSALONIANS 5:9–10** NLT

How does this verse connect to or support what you've learned about God and the plan for salvation?

 Pray about it . . .

- Admit to God that you are a sinner in need of grace. Admit that you cannot take the punishment your sins deserve nor could you ever be good enough to live a life of perfection like God wants.

- Tell God that you believe Jesus died on the cross and rose from the dead for you, personally, to pay the penalty your sin deserves.

- Thank him for being fair and just and loving.

- Tell someone else that you believe this—a parent, a friend, your youth leader, anyone. God is doing amazing things in your heart; tell others about it.

Do You Know What She Did? I Can't Forgive That.

Relationships

When they came to the place called the Skull, they crucified him there, along with the criminals—one on his right, the other on his left. Jesus said, "Father, forgive them, for they do not know what they are doing." And they divided up his clothes by casting lots.

Luke 23:33–34

Have you noticed that things get more complicated the older you get? Remember how you used to fight with a sibling over toys? Or with your friends about what to do at recess—whether to play house or swing, such difficult choices. When a parent or teacher found out you were arguing, they told you to say sorry and then share or compromise. It was all so easy.

Things are so much harder now, aren't they? You no longer fight over toys or recess activities, but the conflict hasn't just disappeared. It's actually a lot more complicated now, isn't it?

Now you're competing with friends for spots on a team. You're arguing about who to be friends with, who to *let* sit by you at lunch. You're learning the power of words and just how awful they can make someone feel. You're learning that being hurt and hurting others cuts deeply. And handling that hurt is so much harder than when you were little and your parents and teachers made you say sorry.

"Sorry," you'd spit through gritted teeth, when all you really wanted to do was smack your sister.

"I'm sorry," you'd say in a singsong voice with a little smile. Within minutes, you'd be playing again, forgetting what you were fighting over in the first place.

Even if you didn't mean it, *sorry* would be said and life would go on.

It doesn't work that way anymore, though, does it? The offenses and conflicts are so much bigger now. The hurt and pain so much deeper. The anger so much stronger. Fake forgiveness isn't enough anymore.

And still, God tells us to forgive.

But you have no idea what she did to me. She made the whole school hate me. She posted that *online. She embarrassed me in a way that no one will ever forget. She said awful things about me and the people I love. She is the problem. She hasn't even asked for forgiveness.*

You're right. I don't know anything about your specific situation. But God does. And still, he tells you to forgive.

So how do you extend forgiveness even when you don't feel like it?

You focus more on Jesus than the person or the pain. As Jesus hung on the cross, surrounded by the soldiers who had literally nailed him there, he prayed, "Father, forgive them, for they do not know what they are doing" (Luke 23:34).

Now, the Bible doesn't clearly lay out who "them" is referring to, but many Bible scholars assume Jesus was asking God to forgive the soldiers who had put him there.

Did they ask for forgiveness?

Did they know how deeply they hurt Jesus?

Did they understand the full impact of what they had done?

No.

And maybe that's the case in your situation too. Fake forgiveness won't erase the bitterness, anger, and resentment that fills your heart, but God can.

Even true forgiveness won't *fix* the other person—it won't take away what she's done or remove it from your memory—but real forgiveness can free your heart.

If you don't feel like you can forgive, ask God to do it for you. And remember that Jesus hung on that cross to forgive all sins, and that means *hers* too.

 Think about it . . .

In one of my favorite books of all time, *The Traveler's Gift* by Andy Andrews, you'll find this question:

> Have you ever been so angry or upset with someone that all you could think of was that person and the horrible way you'd been treated? You think about him when you should be sleeping, and all the things you should have said or would like to say come to mind. . . . That person who offended you is receiving all your energy. You feel as if you might explode.[1]

Can you relate to this? Tell me about a time when someone has offended you and all your energy turned to anger.

Now look how Andrews continues this thought later in the chapter:

> I cannot recall a single book, including the Holy Bible, that says in order for you to forgive someone, he or she has to ask for it. Think

about this concept! Where is the rule written that before I forgive people, they have to deserve it? Where is it written that to be forgiven by me, you must have wronged me no more than three times? Or seven? Or seventeen?

The unmistakable truth about forgiveness is that it is not a reward that must be earned; forgiveness is a gift to be given. When I give forgiveness, I free my own spirit to release the anger and hatred harbored in my heart.[2]

How can forgiving someone else benefit you? What kind of heart does God want you to have, and how can forgiveness help you build that kind of heart?

Be kind and compassionate to one another, forgiving each other, just as in Christ God forgave you.

EPHESIANS 4:32

How does this verse connect to or support what you've learned about forgiveness?

 Pray about it . . .

- Tell God about anyone you are struggling to forgive and what they did to you.

- Admit that you don't feel like forgiving them and that you know unforgiveness is wrong.

- Ask God to forgive that person and to help you do the same.

- Thank him for the grace and forgiveness he offers you every day.

- Ask him to change your heart and make it more like his.

Saying I'm Sorry Isn't Enough

Living

> They [the disciples] went out and preached that people should repent.
>
> Mark 6:12

I hate you!" my twelve-year-old screamed to his seven-month-old baby brother, who looked back at him with a big grin revealing two bottom teeth that had just poked through his gums.

"You're trash!" he yelled as he tickled his brother's belly. The baby responded with giggles.

Before you think my twelve-year-old is evil, let me explain. He was doing a little experiment. He heard somewhere that dogs respond to the tone of voice no matter what words are spoken, and he wondered if the same was true of babies. So he yelled mean words—with a smile on his face and excitement in his tone. Sure enough, his tone of excitement and the smile on his face overpowered the mean words coming out of his mouth.

Could it be that the same is true in other situations? Could it be that our words don't matter as much as the tone with which they're said or the heart behind them?

You've likely grown up being told to apologize:

You hit your brother, say you're sorry.

You were rude to the teacher, say you're sorry.

You were disrespectful to your dad, say you're sorry.

You offended a friend, say you're sorry.

You broke the picture frame, say you're sorry.

I don't even think it's possible to count the number of *I'm sorry*s you've said. But I'm willing to bet you can count the number of *I'm sorry*s you've *felt*.

You know what I'm talking about, don't you? The time you said "I'm sorry" and wanted to cry because it hurt so much. That time you felt so awful about what you had done that you desperately wanted to take it back. That time you knew there was no changing what had happened, and you weren't sure how to move past it, but you knew you never wanted to do that again.

There's another word for that feeling—it's *repentance*. The word *repent* comes from the Greek word *metanoeó*, which means "to change one's mind or purpose."[1] Repentance is an *I'm sorry* connected to a commitment to change.

The words *I'm sorry* are meaningless without the tone of repentance behind them. Apologizing with a tone of repentance results in change. It doesn't just mean you're sorry; it means you're sorry *and* you will put forth effort to turn from the wrong you have done.

If you hit your brother, repentance looks like asking God to help you refrain from acting on your anger and taking deep, calming breaths instead.

If you were rude to the teacher, repentance looks like asking God to give you a heart to see the hard work he or she does and maybe even thank him or her for that.

If you were disrespectful to your dad, repentance looks like looking into his eyes and asking for forgiveness, understanding that God has commanded you to honor your father and mother.

If you offended a friend, repentance looks like asking for and accepting forgiveness and then moving forward, committing to love her well.

If you broke the picture frame, repentance looks like making it right, offering to pay for or fix the frame, and no longer doing what caused it to break.

I'm sorry is so much easier than repentance, but God doesn't instruct us to live a life full of empty *I'm sorrys*. He commands us to repent and turn from our sins so that we may live to bring glory to him.

✳ Think about it . . .

When was the last time you *felt* an *I'm sorry*? Did you take action to change or make it right? If so, what did you do, and what impact did it have? If not, is there something you could do now?

When was the last time you were the recipient of an *I'm sorry* that felt *empty*? How do you know it was empty? What effect did that have on your relationship with or opinion of that person?

> **In the same way, I tell you, there is rejoicing in the presence of the angels of God over one sinner who repents.**
>
> **LUKE 15:10**

How does this verse connect to or support what you've learned about *I'm sorry* and repentance?

 Pray about it . . .

- Thank God for helping you better understand repentance.

- Admit any empty *I'm sorry*s the Holy Spirit has put on your mind, and ask God for forgiveness and for help in turning from that sin and making it right.

- Thank God for the gift of grace and forgiveness.

Is Being a Christian the Same as Being Religious?

I graduated from high school with twenty-eight people. We merged into one class when we were in ninth grade; before that, we were divided into three schools. I went to a church school in the country (there were three kids in my grade). There was a different church school in town, where the class sizes were a little bigger. And then there was the public school, also in town

(I had no idea if or where those kids went to church, but there was at least one more church in our small town).

Before high school, when we came together to play on sports teams or in 4-H groups, we were known by which church we attended: the Trinity kids, the St. John's kids, or the public kids.

Religion was our identity. It was an easy way of classifying each other—and that little piece of information seemed to say a whole lot about who we were.

Even today, people will often ask me what religion I am. But I've learned that the type of church I go to doesn't define me. I could walk through the doors of the same church every single Sunday (or Saturday night), or I could rotate through a variety of doors throughout my life. The church I attend isn't my faith identity—my relationship with Jesus as my personal Savior is. Church and faith are not the same. Religion is different from relationship.

When I meet Jesus in heaven, I don't think he'll be asking which church I went to, searching for my name on some list. Instead, I think he'll look at me like he's known me my whole life, grab my shoulders with his nail-pierced hands, and say, "I'm so glad you're here."

Over the next four weeks, we're going to learn a little more about who Jesus is and how a relationship with him is different from religion.

Want a Relationship with Jesus? Let's Get to Know Him

God

> Though he [Jesus] was God, he did not think of equality with God as something to cling to. Instead, he gave up his divine privileges; he took the humble position of a slave and was born as a human being. When he appeared in human form, he humbled himself in obedience to God and died a criminal's death on a cross.
>
> Philippians 2:6–8 NLT

At the beginning of the year, teachers spend time getting to know you and helping you get to know your classmates. They might have you play some icebreaker games, fill in a bingo sheet, or worse . . . write a few paragraphs or a poem about yourself. I know these activities sometimes feel kind of silly, especially if you already know your classmates well. But those teachers have a purpose: *they* are trying to get to know a whole new group of students, and these games are often more effective than simply asking, "Who are you?" twenty times.

The reality is that at this age, you might struggle to answer the question *Who are you?* It's hard to say, because you're still trying to figure that out.

That's a part of this growing-up process—learning how to become your own person, to figure out who you are.

That's yet one more thing that sets Jesus apart from us. He has always known who he is. He had to go through every stage of life that you do, and he never questioned who he was. From the very beginning, he has always known the answer. An answer we can be sure of. An answer that never changes.

Who is Jesus? He is God and Savior.

Jesus gave up life as a divine being to come to earth as a baby—helpless and dependent. He has all authority on heaven and earth, the power to do mighty works, and he set it all aside to become a baby. A baby who couldn't do a single thing for himself. A baby who fully relied on his mother to keep him alive. He *chose* helplessness over power.

Jesus grew out of the baby phase, just as you did. He learned to walk, he learned to talk, he went to school, he went through puberty (kind of crazy to think of the voice of God with the same awkward, squeaky tone you hear in some of the guys at school, right?). He wasn't born a baby and then suddenly became a man (that's kind of what it feels like when we read the Bible). Though we don't get many details about Jesus's childhood and life as a teenager, we know they happened. Jesus *chose* to walk through *every* phase of human life from birth to adulthood.

Jesus lived with real people. He healed real people. He taught and preached to real people. Sometimes it's hard to understand that. I wish my great-great somebody could tell me stories of what it was like to live with Jesus. How cool would that be? *Back when Jesus and I were young, we walked to school uphill, in the snow, both ways* . . .

While we can't sit down and listen to someone tell us about "that time Jesus . . . ," we can read about his life in the Bible. We can read the words from people who walked beside him and get a glimpse of what it was like to live with Jesus. He *chose* to live with real people like you and me and experience real—human—life with them.

Finally, Jesus died—not just any death, but death on the cross. He was crucified as a criminal, bearing the weight of sins he never committed. Suffering for wrongs he never did. He was punished for lying, talking back, gossiping, treating others poorly, mumbling ugly words, lashing out in anger, rolling eyes in disrespect, stealing, cheating on homework, being rude . . . but he never did a single one of those things. Though he lived a perfect life with not one single sin written beneath his name, he endured the wrath of God for each sin you and I have done and will do. He *chose* to take the punishment we deserve because it was part of his Father's plan of redemption.

Who is Jesus? He is our God, who chose to give up his heavenly privileges in order to live and die as a man—all for you and me.

✳ Think about it . . .

Though Jesus experienced the physical limitations of being human during childhood, as a man, when he began to teach, he had the full power of God to do miracles. You've likely heard of many—changing water into wine, healing the blind, raising Lazarus from the dead, the feeding of the 5,000 (just to name a few)—but if you want a longer list, google "miracles of Jesus." Which of Jesus's miracles impresses you most? If you could have witnessed any of them in person, which would you choose?

Do your best to answer the question *Who are you?* (knowing that your answer is currently in the process of changing and forming).

Write three to five "I am" statements in response. I am . . .

> One day Jesus left the crowds to pray alone. Only his disciples were with him, and he asked them, "Who do people say I am?"
>
> "Well," they replied, "some say John the Baptist, some say Elijah, and others say you are one of the other ancient prophets risen from the dead."
>
> Then he asked them, "But who do you say I am?"
>
> Peter replied, "You are the Messiah sent from God!"
>
> LUKE 9:18–20 NLT

How does this verse connect to or support what you've learned about who Jesus is?

 Pray about it . . .

- Tell Jesus who you think he is.

- Thank Jesus for all the things he chose to do: give up power to become a baby, child, and teenager; live with real people; suffer and die for our sins.

- Admit that it can be hard to really *know* Jesus.

- Ask the Holy Spirit to help you get to know Jesus better and understand him more by reading the Bible.

Your Faith Is Yours

Self

For God so loved the world that he gave his one and only Son,
that whoever believes in him shall not perish but have eternal life.

John 3:16

I grew up going to church. I went to a small church school. I was baptized as a baby. I was confirmed as an eighth grader. I did all the church things.

Sure, I knew about God. I believed he created the world in seven days. I imagined what it would have been like to see him part the Red Sea as Moses held up his arms. I thought about how awful it would have been to be stuck in the belly of a fish for three days like Jonah. I knew all the stories.

I knew about Jesus too. I thought about how cool it would have been to be at the wedding where he turned water into wine. Or to eat from the loaves of bread and fish that he miraculously multiplied. I appreciated the work he did on the cross, but I didn't like to think about the gruesomeness of it all. I remember singing "I know that my redeemer lives" on Easter morning. I knew all the words.

I knew about salvation. That it was by faith you were saved. That all have sinned and fallen short of the glory of God. That it was by Christ's wounds you were healed. That it was finished on the cross. I knew all the verses.

I knew *about* all those things, but I didn't really *know* God. I didn't really put all my faith in what Jesus had done. I didn't have the Holy Spirit living within me.

Because everything I knew was about religion—not about relationship.

When I learned that God wanted a relationship with me, it changed everything. I wasn't saved because I went to Sunday school or a Christian school. I wasn't saved because of church customs I had participated in. I wasn't saved because my family went to church or because my parents told me I was a Christian.

I am saved because I believe in Jesus with my whole heart.

I believe that God sent his Son—with all the power and authority of God—to be born as a baby.

For *me*.

I believe that when God was talking with Adam and Eve about their sin, he already had a plan to redeem the world.

To redeem *me*.

I believe that when Jesus hung on the cross, he paid for the sins of all who believe in him.

My pride and disrespect and nasty words and awful thoughts and desire for control weighed down his body as he took his last breath and said, "It is finished."

I believe that the tomb was empty, and now the same power that raised Jesus from the dead is given to every believer through the Holy Spirit. Given to *me*.

Faith isn't something you get just from showing up. Salvation isn't passed down from mother to daughter. Belief doesn't come from memorizing and reciting words.

A relationship with Jesus begins in *your* heart. It's *your* faith. Salvation is a gift offered to *you* specifically—*your* name was on Jesus's mind as he hung on the cross. The evidence of believing in Jesus is seen in *your* life.

Sweet girl, this faith is *yours*. Claim it. Grab hold of it. Delight in it. Live it out.

Think about it ...

Imagine your mom or dad or someone else who has been important in guiding your faith standing next to you with a sponge. They've carried this sponge with them their whole life; it's full of water (and all kinds of other stuff) that has been soaked up along the way.

You have your own sponge. It's brand new and clean and dry. If your mom squeezes out her sponge into yours, whose water does your sponge soak up? Is your sponge now full of water that has been soaked up during *your* life? Or is it full of water that has been soaked up during that person's life?

How can this relate to faith and its ability to be passed on to the people we love? Can personal faith be passed on?

Let's keep thinking about this "faith" sponge. If you want it to be full of your own water (your own faith), you have to use it in your own life, right? But a dry sponge doesn't really soak anything up; it just moves the things it touches around. For the sponge to soak things up, it must be wet. Who or where should you go to fill your sponge? How do you think you do that?

> Jesus answered her, "If you knew the gift of God and who it is
> [Jesus] that asks you for a drink, you would have asked him and he
> would have given you living water."
>
> JOHN 4:10

How does this verse connect to or support what you've learned about the
sponge of personal faith?

 ## Pray about it . . .

- Tell God that you want your own faith, and explain the specific ways
  you've been trying to soak up other people's faith.

- Thank him for being a personal God who wants a relationship with *you.*

- Admit that you haven't always understood this idea of personal faith and
  maybe still don't.

- Ask God to grow your faith and help you soak up the living water from
  Jesus and make your faith your own.

I'm Tired of Feeling Powerless

Relationships

Jesus replied, "Truly I tell you, the Son is not able to do anything on his own, but only what he sees the Father doing. For whatever the Father does, the Son likewise does these things. For the Father loves the Son and shows him everything he is doing, and he will show him greater works than these so that you will be amazed."

John 5:19–20 CSB

Do you ever feel like your whole life is being controlled by someone else? Like you have to ask permission for *everything*. Like you get to make *zero* decisions on your own. It doesn't matter whether you're at school or at home; someone else is always in charge.

Do you ever find yourself thinking *I can't wait until I'm older, then I can . . .*

Go to the bathroom without asking.

Sit wherever I want.

Stay up as late as I want.

Sleep as long as I want.

Get whatever apps I want.

Do whatever I want.

This age is hard because you begin to realize what little power you have and feel like you deserve more. After all, you're not a little kid anymore; you are ready to make your own choices.

Jesus gets it.

I know what you're thinking . . . *Wait a second. Jesus was God—He had ALL the power. He could do whatever he wanted. Yeah, I know he lived as a human, I know he was once twelve, but still, he was God. He could do whatever he wanted if he wanted to. I mean, he turned water into wine and raised dead people.*

You're right. He did have the power of God. But Jesus didn't use that power to simply do whatever he wanted. During his time on earth, Jesus did exactly and only what he knew his Father's will was. He stayed within the boundaries of God's will because it was also his will. He *wanted* to do what his Father wanted him to do.

Jesus didn't walk around the Holy Land using his power to make life easier or more fun—making food instantaneously appear before him, teleporting from one city to the next, turning annoying people into toads.

Even Jesus surrendered to his Father's will, using his power only on what they agreed was right. Jesus and his Father were on the same team.

Your parents are on your team too.

Jesus shows us what it looks like to respect our parents, to trust their boundaries, to accept their limitations of our power, and to work with them to do what is right.

Now, it's important to understand that your parents (or any adults in your life) are not God. They are not holy and perfect and just. They will make mistakes. But it's also important to know that God has placed relationships with adults in your life to help guide you. He has chosen them to help you learn how to make your own choices. And, ultimately, God—as your Heavenly Father—wants to help you make those choices and teach you to use power well.

I hate that I have to include this, but not all adults are trustworthy. Not all choose to submit to God's will. There are adults in this world who misuse their power and authority in harmful ways. If an adult is leading you into sin, acting in a way that opposes God's instructions for life in the Bible, or is harming you—God's beloved daughter—that adult is wrong. God does not give permission to harm others or sin just because someone is an *adult.* You do not need to surrender to adults who are not surrendering to God. If there is a dangerous adult in your life, tell someone. I'm praying right now that God will give you the courage and strength to speak up.

Think about it . . .

If you could have the power to do *anything* right now, what would you do? Would using power in this way honor God? Would Jesus have used his power in this way?

Who are the adults in your life who seem to limit your power and restrict your choices? What specific limitations bother you? Are these limitations there to protect you? Why or why not? What would it look like for you to be on the same team concerning these limitations? Are there any limits you'd like to talk to them about? If so, what do you want to say to them?

> **For I [Jesus] have come down from heaven to do the will of God who sent me, not to do my own will.**
>
> JOHN 6:38 NLT

How does this verse connect to or support what you've learned about Jesus this week?

 Pray about it . . .

- Tell God that it is hard to feel like you have no power.

- Ask him to help you be obedient and accept limits from the adults he's placed in your life; ask him to help you respectfully talk with those adults about your desire to make some of your own choices.

- Tell God that you want to make choices that follow *his* will.

- Thank God for sending Jesus to teach us how to work as a team with our parents and other adults, and thank Jesus for sacrificing life in heaven to come to this earth to show us how to live well as humans.

How Do I Make Room for God Every Day?

Living

Come near to God and he will come near to you.

James 4:8a

Have you ever experienced something that you wish would last forever? A day on the lake, an afternoon full of shopping and pedicures with friends, the moment when the buzzer sounded and you won the game, a special memory with a loved one. If you could, you'd start every single day like that because it would make the rest of your day a little sweeter.

I feel that way about church. Sometimes I sit there on Sunday mornings and wish I could start every day like that. I know, I'm weird. My kids tell me that all the time. But really, I do.

I didn't always feel this way. I remember sitting in the church pew, checking my watch, wondering how much longer it would last. I remember daydreaming as I listened to bold baritone voices blend with high-pitched, almost opera-like tones. I remember thinking that I was glad we only did this once a week.

But here's what I'm learning now and want so badly to tell you: Jesus isn't *just* found in church. God isn't confined to a sanctuary or a building. We can live every single day, every single moment with him.

So how do you do this? What does it look like to live every day with Jesus?

First of all, you've already got a great start because you're working through this book. You're taking time out of your day to spend time with him. You're learning more about God, what he says about you, and how he wants you to live. If you want to live every day with Jesus, you simply need to spend time with him. Here are some more practical ways you can spend time with God.

Pray.

Not just recited words but short little thoughts throughout your day. When you're stressed out about a test: "God, help me stay calm and do my best. Please help me feel confident that my best is good enough." When you are annoyed with someone: "God, remind me that this person is fearfully and wonderfully made, and help me show your love." When you feel alone: "God, I know you are my friend and that you fill my heart, but I'm really lonely. Please send me a friend." Prayer doesn't have to be complicated; it just has to be from your heart.

Listen.

Turn on some Christian music as you're getting ready for school. Ask your mom or dad to find a Christian station for the drive, or if you have earbuds and a phone, listen on the bus. Maybe turn it on just before going to bed to help focus your thoughts before trying to fall asleep. Make Christian music part of your daily routine.

Read.

You're already reading this book (and I'm so happy you are!), but don't forget to read the Bible too. My words should never replace God's Word. If you have a phone, you can use the Bible app on it and read the verse of the day each morning before leaving the house. You could ask your mom or dad to read a few verses with you at night. Or listen to an audio version of the Bible. Don't stress out about how much to read or needing a specific plan. Simply show up and open the Bible so you can connect with God through his Word.

 Think about it . . .

What are you already doing to spend time with God every day? There are other ways to connect with God I haven't talked about—can you think of more? Is there anything you'd like to add to your routine? What will that look like? When will you do it?

Think about your best friend or maybe a really important adult in your life. What would happen if that person moved away? How would you stay connected? What would happen if you stopped doing those things? How would the lack of communication and connection impact your relationship? How might this situation apply to our relationship with God?

> These commandments that I give you today are to be on your hearts. Impress them on your children. Talk about them when you sit at home and when you walk along the road, when you lie down and when you get up.
>
> **DEUTERONOMY 6:6–7**

How does this verse connect to or support what you've learned about connecting with God every day?

 *Pray about it . . .*

- Thank God for always being available and for inviting you into a personal relationship with him through Jesus's death on the cross.

- Admit that you forget to spend time with him and sometimes don't make it a priority.

- Ask God to help you find ways to connect with him every day throughout your day.

How Do I Fight Sin and Temptation?

"Fight, fight, fight . . ." I laughed a little and rolled my eyes as a group of fourth-grade boys chanted. Their eyes were fixed on two gibbons that had climbed to the top of their enclosure. The boys were on a field trip to the zoo. The gibbons, maybe encouraged by the boys' chanting, were clawing at each other, fighting for a place at the top of the climbing pole. Each hung by one (extremely flexible) arm, using the other arm as well as their legs to swipe at the opposite gibbon dangling from the net, which kept them from swinging into the wild of the zoo.

Fight—it seems to be a natural instinct for boys, doesn't it? Maybe you've witnessed this? Between siblings? Between class-mates who are boys? Sometimes it's silly, but sometimes it can be downright mean.

Though this deep desire to fight seems more aggressive and instinctive in boys, we girls have it too. We like to think girls fight for what's right, fight for equality, fight for a seat at the table.

Over these next few weeks, I'm going to encourage you to fight a different kind of fight. I want you to fight sin, tempta-tion, and the devil. And the whole time, I hope you imagine me standing next to you, cheering, "Fight, fight, fight . . ." because I believe in our God, who is stronger than sin, temptation, and the devil. And I believe he will give you the power to fight all that opposes him.

Is Satan Real?

God

> Stay alert! Watch out for your great enemy, the devil. He prowls around like a roaring lion, looking for someone to devour. Stand firm against him, and be strong in your faith. Remember that your family of believers all over the world is going through the same kind of suffering you are.
>
> 1 Peter 5:8–9 NLT

The devil made me do it." I don't remember the first time I heard these words—maybe in the comics section of the Sunday newspaper that sat next to my grandpa's chair. Even as a kid, those simple words prompted some deep thinking. *Does the devil really have that much power? Isn't Satan just a cartoon figure—the creepy but kind of cute little red guy with horns, a tail, and a pitchfork? Can the devil really make me do things I don't want to do? Is he actually real?*

Years later, sitting in a Bible study, I contemplated those questions again. Once more, I found myself wondering if the devil is a fictional character created to teach kids about right and wrong or if he actually exists, lurking in the unseen, trying his best to lead us toward wrong.

Here's what I learned: the devil is, indeed, very real—and very active. The Bible is clear about his existence. We see him in the form of the snake that tempts Eve, we see him throughout the Old Testament as one who opposes God, and the New Testament writers warn believers about his sneakiness. There is no doubt: Satan (also known as the devil, the tempter, the accuser, the roaring lion) does exist.

So what do we do with that? How do we move our understanding from a cartoon image of the devil to accepting the fact that he is a real and evil presence in our lives?

Priscilla Shirer says it like this: "The enemy may be invisible, but he is not fictional."[1] Your enemy is real, and he exists to lead you away from God, just like he did to our sister Eve so long ago.

Sometimes I think we get caught up in a list of sins, scanning the Bible for the things we're not supposed to do. We want a black-and-white list of rules: do this, don't do that. But so often we find ourselves in the gray area.

Well, if I do this, I'm not *technically* breaking a commandment. The Bible doesn't exactly say anything about vaping. Nowhere does it say, "Thou shalt not have TikTok or Snapchat." Our world is far different from that of Eve's or Moses's or Jesus's, but God's Word is everlasting and can be applied in *every* century.

The heart of the devil is to oppose God. Think back to the Garden of Eden. God told Adam not to eat the fruit "from the tree of the knowledge of good and evil" (Genesis 2:17). The serpent (aka the devil) tempted Eve by turning her heart toward doubt; he led her to want something that opposed what God wanted for her. "Did God really say, 'You must not eat from any tree in the garden'?" the serpent asked (Genesis 3:1).

When you are stuck in a gray area, the devil does the same to you. He drops thoughts into your mind. *Did **you** really think God said that? Are **you** sure this is wrong? Does the Bible specifically say **you** shouldn't do this? Is this what **you** want? Wouldn't God want **you** to be happy?*

Who are these questions focused on? Satan wants you to look away from God and toward yourself. He knows that if you're thinking about *you*, he can get you to do what *he* wants. And he knows that if you keep your focus on God and ask for strength, God will lead you out of temptation (see Matthew 6:13).

When you're stuck in that gray area and notice that all your attention is on you, fight the devil's questions with some of your own, questions that focus on God. *Does this contradict **God's plan** for his people? Would this hurt **God's heart**? Does this **bring glory to God**? Will this make me more **like Jesus**?*

The devil is real. Temptation is real. But God is also real. And he has already won the war against the devil through Jesus's death on the cross. And because of that, you can fight daily battles of temptation with the same power that raised Jesus from the dead. Keep your focus on God, and ask questions that include his name. Stand firm and be strong in your faith.

✳ Think about it . . .

Think about that cartoon image of the devil. Does that image help you understand the reality of the devil? Why or why not? How would you explain the devil's influence on girls (and boys) your age? What are some of the biggest temptations you face? Remember that you have the same power that raised Jesus from the dead within you, available to help you fight temptation. What does that power look like, and what kind of image could represent that? Maybe you could sketch an image of the power of God as a visual reminder for the next time you face one of those temptations.

What's a gray area you've been stuck in lately? Something that has you wondering whether or not God would approve. Maybe it's something you're personally struggling with, maybe a friend is going through it, or maybe it's something the world says is okay but you're not sure about. Explain the gray area here and then ask those God-focused questions. Answer as many as you can with evidence from the Bible. If you don't know the answers, ask an older faith-friend for help.

> For we are not fighting against flesh-and-blood enemies, but against evil rulers and authorities of the unseen world, against mighty powers in this dark world, and against evil spirits in the heavenly places.
>
> **EPHESIANS 6:12 NLT**

How does this verse connect to or support what you've learned about the devil and temptation?

 *Pray about it . . .*

- Ask God to help you understand the reality of the devil and to open your eyes to how Satan is working against you.

- Tell God about the things that are tempting you right now.

- Admit that you aren't strong enough to resist temptation on your own or even to recognize when something goes against God's plan.

- Ask God to help you see temptation and to resist it in his strength.

- Thank God for his faithfulness, his power, his presence, and his forgiveness.

But How Do I Actually Fight Sin?

Self

And we are instructed to turn from godless living and sinful pleasures. We should live in this evil world with wisdom, righteousness,
and devotion to God . . .

Titus 2:12 NLT

Parents are annoying, aren't they? They say things like . . .

Back when I was a kid, I talked to my friends on the phone with a land-
line (whatever that is) instead of texting them.

I didn't have my own device when I was in sixth grade; we didn't even
have cell phones.

I wrote essays on paper—in cursive—not typed on a computer or tablet.

It's like they lived in a totally different world than you do. And that's kind
of true. Their worlds were a *lot* different from the one you're growing up in,
so sometimes their stories and rules and expectations reflect that.

You know what's crazy about the Bible? Even though it was written almost
two thousand years ago, during a time period and world completely foreign

to you, God designed it to be just as relevant today as it was then. So when you read words like "We should live in this evil world," that *evil world* is referring not only to the world of the AD 60s (when the book of Titus was written), but it's also referring to *today*, right now, *this* evil world.

God's Word is alive and active (see Hebrews 4:12). The Bible is our guide for life *now*. God inspired Paul's writing with you in mind, with the present world in mind. He knew the challenges you would face in the twenty-first century, even thousands of years before you were born. He knew you would face the temptations of "godless living and sinful pleasures," and he knew exactly what they would look like.

The world is full of temptations: sexual sin, porn, drugs, alcohol misuse, rudeness, selfishness, disobedience to parents, negative attitudes, laziness, irresponsibility, inappropriate shows and music—the list goes on and on.

If I had asked you to list examples of godless living or sinful pleasures, you might have included those first few (sexual sin, porn, drugs, alcohol misuse)—they are givens on the "ungodly" list. But as you read through the other examples, you may have begun to feel a little uneasy. Maybe you hadn't thought of rudeness, disobedience to parents, laziness, or inappropriate shows and music as examples of godless living or sinful pleasures.

When God inspired Paul to write the words "live in this evil world with wisdom, righteousness, and devotion to God" (Titus 2:12 NLT), he knew you'd be reading them. He knew the temptations you'd face. He knew they'd be different from those of Titus and the people of Crete in the 60s (the AD 60s), different from those your parents faced, and different from those your some-day children will face. Yet God's command is the same: to live with wisdom, righteousness, and devotion to God.

So how do you do that? How do you resist temptation? You ask God for *HELP*.
Honor God

When you face temptation, and you start to feel like something is wrong, ask yourself, *Does this honor God? Would I do this with Jesus sitting next to me?* If the answer is yes, then go for it. If it's no, then . . .

Escape plan

Ask God to provide an escape plan, a way out, an exit strategy.

Practically, this might look like walking away, saying no to an invitation where you know you'll be tempted, or texting your parent a secret code (maybe an X) that says you need an excuse to get out of there and to call you with one right away.

If your escape plan works, praise God for providing. If not . . .

Learn from it

So you messed up. The temptation overwhelmed you, you didn't see a way out, and you sinned. Learn from it. First, repent (we talked about that in week 24) and ask God for forgiveness. And then . . .

Prepare for next time

The devil knows your weakness, and he's going to put that temptation in front of you again. Ask God to help you prepare for it. Maybe even write out some possible escape plans so that you're ready the next time the devil dangles the temptation in front of you.

Check out page 281 in the back of this book for a flowchart version of how to ask God for HELP. It has easy-to-follow yes or no questions to help you fight sin.

❋ Think about it . . .

Make a list of all the ways your parents' world growing up was different from your world. (Ask them what decade they were in as a twelve-year-old, and google what life was like then. Better yet, ask them what life was like.) Make a second list of ways their world and your world are the same.

What are some examples of things that tempt you into godless living and sinful pleasures? Which are the hardest to resist? Why?

> **The temptations in your life are no different from what others experience. And God is faithful. He will not allow the temptation to be more than you can stand. When you are tempted, he will show you a way out so that you can endure.**
>
> **1 CORINTHIANS 10:13 NLT**

How does this verse connect to or support what you've learned about temptation?

 *Pray about it . . .*

- Tell God about the temptations you face.

- Thank him for being near you during them.

- Admit the times you have failed in the past, and ask for forgiveness.

- Ask him to help you escape current temptations and prepare you for future ones.

- Thank God for giving you the Bible, which is relevant for *all* of time, not just the time when it was written.

Fighting the Temptation to Weaponize Your Words

Relationships

The words of the reckless pierce like swords, but the tongue of the wise brings healing.

Proverbs 12:18

"You're trash," my son said to his sister. My son is three. My three-year-old called his big sister trash. Why? Because he heard his big brother (jokingly) call a friend trash as they played video games.

If you have younger siblings, you know they're like little parrots. If they hear you say a word, they'll use that word too. If you don't have younger siblings, imagine having a bright red, yellow, and blue bird always sitting on your shoulder, listening to every word, and then repeating most of what you say—the good and the bad.

Here's some advice about how to watch your language. Live your life as if a preschooler is behind you every second of the day. Choose your words as if you will soon hear them come out of a three-year-old's mouth.

You understand the power of words, though. After all, you are a middle school girl. You have likely been called names, had rumors spread about you, or maybe been the name caller or rumor spreader.

Throughout the Bible, God illustrates the power of language. In Psalm 57:4b, the psalmist writes about "men whose teeth are spears and arrows, whose tongues are sharp swords." Another comparison between words and weapons is found in Proverbs 25:18: "Like a club or a sword or a sharp arrow is one who gives false testimony against a neighbor." These verses prove the power of our words. Power, however, can be used for good or for evil.

It looks like you have a choice to make. You can either use your words to build up and encourage others or as weapons to tear down and destroy. It's an easy choice, right? Obviously, you would rather build up and encourage than tear down and destroy. But the action—actually resisting the temptation to use harsh words—that's a whole lot harder.

Controlling the power of your words isn't a solo mission because what God wants you to do, he will equip you to do. With practice, you can allow your words to be motivated and monitored by your Savior. Maybe instead of imagining a parrot on your shoulder, you can imagine Jesus by your side.

Do you recall any stories in the Bible when Jesus used foul language when things didn't go his way? Did he ever use God's name carelessly? After hanging out with Peter, did he go to John and complain about how annoying Peter was? Did he use different words around his friends than he did around his Father? Remember, Jesus is our teacher, showing us how to live, and because of our faith in him, we've been given the gift of the Holy Spirit, who helps us live like Jesus. When we ask him, the Holy Spirit can give us patience and gentleness when we feel annoyed. He can give us wisdom to know when to speak and when to be silent. He can guide our words to be kind even when we have to say hard things.

On our journey to live like Jesus and follow in his footsteps, we must make our words a priority and ask the Holy Spirit for help.

The next time your words threaten to catapult out like spears or arrows, take a moment to ask the Holy Spirit to guide you and use your words for good, not destruction. When anger and annoyance tempt you to use your words as a club, to beat someone down, ask him to help you stop and see that person from the view of God's love. Ask him to transform your words from weapons to support beams, building up those around you.

 Think about it . . .

Do you speak more words than you type or text? Really. Think about that for a minute. How does most of your communication happen? Face-to-face or from screen to screen? Which option (face or screen) makes it easier to use words as weapons, to say hurtful things? Why? What practical things could you do to remind yourself to use words well when you're communicating from screen to screen?

There are lots of ways to use your words for good. You could send a text or message of encouragement to a friend. You could write a thank-you on a sticky note and secretly place it somewhere your parent or teacher will see it. You could look someone in the eyes and give them a compliment.

Choose at least one of these to do in the next twenty-four hours. Come back and write down what you did and what the person's reaction was. Explain how it made you feel to use your words well.

> **Do not let any unwholesome talk come out of your mouths, but only what is helpful for building others up according to their needs, that it may benefit those who listen.**
>
> **EPHESIANS 4:29**

How does this verse connect to or support what you've learned about the power of words and how you use them?

 Pray about it . . .

- Tell God about the times you have been hurt by the words of others, and ask him to heal those wounds.

- Admit that you, too, struggle to use your words well sometimes, confess the times you have weaponized your words, and ask for forgiveness and for help to honor him with what you say in person and online.

- Thank God for the gift of language and that he has given us many ways to communicate.

- Ask him to guide your words and to use them to build up and encourage others.

God, Do You Even Care?

Living

> The LORD said to Moses, "I have heard the grumbling of the Isra-
> elites. Tell them, 'At twilight you will eat meat, and in the morning
> you will be filled with bread. Then you will know that I am the
> LORD your God.'"
>
> Exodus 16:11–12

Kelsey, nobody else even cares," my sister cried on the other end of the phone. I couldn't see them, but I'm pretty sure there were tears of frustration. I imagine she was lying on her bed, feet against the wall, feeling like her anger was ready to explode all over her bedspread. She was thirteen. I was twenty-four. She was frustrated with her volleyball team—the other girls didn't seem to care whether they won or lost. In my sister's mind, they weren't trying very hard, and she was over it. I was supposed to make her feel better.

I don't remember exactly what I said to her over the phone that night, but I remember feeling frustrated beside her and wanting so badly to fix it. I've had that same feeling many times in my own life. Except I've been the one crying out, not to my big sister, but to God.

God, do you even care?

Do you care that this world is awful and messed up? Do you care that in-nocent people die? Do you care that I'm hurting? Do you care that our world is confusing and I don't know what to do? Do you care that so-called Christians distort your words, pulling people away from the Truth? Do you care that life is hard? God, do you even care?

It's easy to question the goodness of God when all we see is the badness of the world. We're not the first to experience this. Remember the Israelites? God used the plagues in Egypt (frogs, locusts, and flies, oh my!) to convince Pharaoh to let them out of slavery. Moses led them across the Red Sea on dry land. Remember them?

Not long after their miraculous escape from Egypt, they began grumbling in the wilderness, saying, "If only we had died by the LORD's hand in Egypt! There we sat around pots of meat and ate all the food we wanted, but you have brought us out into this desert to starve this entire assembly to death" (Exodus 16:3). You see, they were hungry (maybe a little hangry) and didn't understand what God was doing. Those words were their version of *God, do you even care?*

And you know what God's response was? He gave them manna—just enough for that day, every day. God's people were starving, so he gave them literal bread from heaven. What if God responds to our grumbling in a similar way?

God, do you even care?

He does, and he gives us manna—just enough for this day.

God, do you even care that there's been another school shooting and I'm scared?

Manna for the day: "And surely I am with you always, to the very end of the age" (Matthew 28:20).

God, do you even care that people are cruel and get away with awful things?

Manna for the day: "Do not fret because of those who are evil or be envious of those who do wrong; for like the grass they will soon wither, like green plants they will soon die away" (Psalm 37:1–2).

God, do you even care that life is hard?

Manna for the day: "In this world you will have trouble. But take heart! I have overcome the world" (John 16:33).

Yes, we live in a messed up, fallen world full of sin, and sometimes it feels like God doesn't even care. But here's the truth: God cares more than we understand, and every moment brings us closer to the perfection of eternity. God will not rid the world of all evil until the day Jesus comes again. But until then, he gives us manna for the day so that we can endure the troubles of this life as we wait with the hope of eternity.

God's not going to solve every problem today, but he will give you what you need to survive them.

Think about it . . .

Write out as many worries and frustrations as you can think of. All the things that complete the cry "God, do you even care . . . ?"

Now pick the one that is most immediate, the one that is making your heart feel heavy today. I want you to tell God about it in prayer. Right now. Pray aloud, "God, do you even care that . . ." And then ask him for manna—to give you what you need to survive the heaviness of that cry. Then, tomorrow, come back to this space and think about how God helped you endure that heaviness. Write about your manna below.

> I heard a loud shout from the throne, saying, "Look, God's home is now among his people! He will live with them, and they will be his people. God himself will be with them. He will wipe every tear from their eyes, and there will be no more death or sorrow or crying or pain. All these things are gone forever."
>
> **REVELATION 21:3–4** NLT

How does this verse connect to or support what you've learned about hard times and the hope of heaven?

 Pray about it . . .

- Admit that you often get overwhelmed by the badness of the world and need help remembering God's goodness.

- Tell God about your worries and frustrations.

- Ask him to give you manna for each of them.

- Thank God for preparing heaven for you, a place of perfection, and for providing hope while you wait to join him there.

What Do I Do with All These Feelings?

I remember my first day of school my sophomore year of high school. I cried. Not because someone was mean to me, not because I hated it, not because it was hard.

I cried because I didn't have homework.

Oh. My. Goodness. I was such a nerd. Looking back, that seems ridiculous. But, looking back, I also understand those tears a little more. I don't think I was crying because I desperately wanted to do math problems or write an essay. I think I cried because I was full of so many emotions, and I just didn't know what to do with them. So I cried.

I have never felt so many emotions in such an overwhelming way as when I was a teenage girl. You get it, right? You feel these giant, unexplained emotions, too, don't you? Please tell me I'm not the only one.

Girl, it gets better. You won't always feel so much and so hard. Your body, brain, and heart will settle down and allow you to feel and process emotions in a calmer way eventually. For now, hang on, because it's sort of a wild ride. And, remember, you're not alone. God's Spirit is within you, and your sisters are beside you (we get it). You're going to be okay.

Over the next four weeks we're going to take a closer look at these emotions, what to do with them, and how our faith impacts the way we respond to them.

Jesus Went through Puberty

God

Every year Jesus' parents went to Jerusalem for the Festival of the Passover. When he was twelve years old, they went up to the festival, according to the custom.

Luke 2:41–42

You have no idea what this feels like. You just don't get it. You don't know what it's like to be me.

Do you ever feel lonely? Like no one else in your life really understands you? It doesn't matter if you have the best parents, lots of friends, or even a sister close to your age; no one has experienced or is experiencing life in the same way you are. And that can feel really lonely.

It would be easy for me to respond to the feelings you're experiencing by speaking some Christianese to you (you know, those cute little sayings that don't really help but sound Christian-like). Something like, "You're never really alone; God is with you all the time."

But I know that would be kind of annoying and probably not helpful. So I won't tell you not to be lonely. I won't remind you that God is with you. Instead, I'm going to show you that Jesus knows how you feel. I'm going to tell you that even in those moments when you feel like no one else understands what you're going through, God knows. And I'm going to remind you that the power of the Holy Spirit lives inside you.

If I asked you to make a timeline of Jesus's life, it might look something like this:

Jesus was born   Jesus taught   Jesus died

Most of the information we have about Jesus's life from the Bible is focused on his ministry, his adult years. It kind of seems like he went from baby to man overnight. And even though we know that's not true, because he came to earth as a human being and must have lived all the years from birth to death, it's really hard to imagine him as anything other than the baby in the manger, the miracle worker, or the man on the cross. Scripture tells us almost nothing about Jesus's childhood and adolescent years. Except for that one spot in Luke: "Every year Jesus' parents went to Jerusalem for the Festival of the Passover. When he was twelve years old, they went up to the festival, according to the custom" (Luke 2:41–42).

Read that again. How old was Jesus when they went to Jerusalem for the Festival of the Passover? Circle his age in the verses above.

Now, write it here: Jesus was _____ years old.

Jesus outgrew childhood.

Jesus went through puberty.

Jesus experienced the physical changes of adolescence.

Jesus experienced the hormonal shifts inside his body.

Jesus experienced all the emotions that come with mental and emotional development.

Jesus *became* an adult; it didn't just happen overnight.

Luke goes on to tell about Jesus being forgotten in Jerusalem and then found days later in the temple. But that's not my point here. I believe every word of the Bible is God-breathed, written by men but inspired by God. Every word.

Luke could have said, "When Jesus was a young man, when he was a child, when he was not yet grown." Or he could have left out the indication of age altogether. But instead, God inspired him to write the words, "When he was twelve years old."

I think he wanted you to read them. I think he wanted you to know that no matter how lonely you feel, there is One who understands. Jesus was once a twelve-year-old too. I know . . . but he wasn't a twelve-year-old *girl*. You're right. But he was a twelve-year-old human. At one point in his life, he was *your* exact age. He understands the human experience of growing from child to teen.

And he is an all-knowing, everlasting God whose Holy Spirit is present within believers every moment of every day, no matter their age. I once heard someone say there is no *junior* Holy Spirit. The same Spirit of God who lives in adult believers also lives in you.

So, when you feel like no one around you *gets* it and you feel alone, I hope you'll remember this: your Savior Jesus walked in teenage shoes, God understands you like no one else ever could because he created your inmost being, and the Holy Spirit has a one-size-fits-all kind of power. Girl, you are not alone, and you are so very loved by a triune God who gets you.

✳ Think about it . . .

What parts of this whole growing-up thing feel the loneliest? What are you going through that no one seems to understand? What are you going through that you don't understand?

If you could sit down with Jesus right now, what questions would you ask him about this stage of life? What would you want to know about his life during this stage?

> You saw me before I was born. Every day of my life was recorded in your book. Every moment was laid out before a single day had passed.
>
> **PSALM 139:16 NLT**

How does this verse connect to or support what you've learned about this phase of life and your connection to God?

 Pray about it . . .

- Tell God the best parts of being a middle school girl and tell him the worst.

- Thank him for sending Jesus to live a complete human life, even that of a twelve-year-old.

- Ask God to help you feel less alone by remembering that Jesus gets you and that the power of the Holy Spirit lives within you.

Why Do I Feel Like I'm Going to Explode?

Self

From the depths of despair, O LORD, I call for your help. Hear my cry, O Lord. Pay attention to my prayer.

Psalm 130:1–2 NLT

Geology has never been my favorite subject. I still can't tell you the difference between sedimentary rocks and igneous ones. I only know what limestone is because it can be found in the pastures and fields I walked through growing up on the farm. I don't know the difference between lava and magma (or is it magna? I'm not even sure). And I definitely can't name all the layers of the earth. I know we live on the surface—that's all that matters, right?

But volcanoes kind of fascinate me. Not in the I-want-to-learn-more-about-them kind of way, but in the wow-those-explosions-are-amazing kind of way. And sometimes in the I-*feel*-like-a-volcano kind of way.

Instead of lava or magma (I told you I didn't know the difference) bubbling up inside me, threatening to explode, I feel like there are emotions building up, ready to burst out.

Anger, sadness, fear, worry. Sometimes excitement, happiness, goofiness, fun. *All* emotions feel really big. And sometimes they explode. They come out in tears or nasty words; they come out in giggles and random squeals. They come out in slammed doors and eye rolls. Or worse yet, sometimes they don't come out at all, and I feel the pressure and tension inside, but there's no way to release it.

So I explode to God. I open my computer and let the words flow onto the keyboard. I take out a piece of paper and let them escape through the pen. I close my eyes and cry silently inside as the tears create hot, sticky streams down my cheeks. I yell at the air and scream into the great big sky. I punch a pillow and then bury my head in it. I explode to God and let all the big, messy emotions erupt onto him.

And you know what he does? He lets them flow right into his arms. He picks up the little pieces of debris left by the big explosion. He opens his arms and reaches for me. And then he holds me. He holds me until I'm empty inside.

And then he fills me up. He urges me to take a long, deep breath and inhale his peace, his love, his calm.

After a few minutes, my insides rest again. The tension fades because the pressure has been released. God loves me the same before the explosion, in the middle of it, and after it has passed.

You don't have to hide your emotions from God. You don't have to pretend things are calm inside when you feel like you're going to explode. You don't have to fake happiness when sadness threatens to consume you. You don't have to say you're fine when your anger is so hot you feel like your cheeks are on fire or the sadness is so intense you feel like you might drown.

Did you know that the Psalms are full of emotional explosions? There are verses about anxiety, depression, longing for God to make his presence known, questions, doubts, sorrow, and fear. One book of the Bible is titled *Lamentations*—a word that means an expression of grief or sorrow. And then there's the book of Job, full of suffering and questioning, so much that at one point Job wonders why he was even born at all (see Job 3:11).

Remember last week when we talked about how every word of the Bible was inspired by God for a purpose? What if the purpose of the verses and books I just mentioned is to help us understand that God can handle our emotional explosions?

Open your heart. Let the emotional lava flow and explode even when you don't know why you feel the way you do. God will listen and offer comfort and love just as he did for the men who wrote the Psalms and Lamentations, and even for Job himself. You don't have to understand your emotions to pour them out to God.

 Think about it . . .

I want you to emotionally explode all over this page. Use a pen or a pencil, crayons, markers, or paint—I don't care. Choose colors that connect with the feelings inside you and let them escape. Use words, images, scribbles, whatever feels right.

Your emotions can feel explosive, right? As your brain and body grow, God created them to adjust and adapt and to release those emotions in healthy ways. We know that real volcanoes can be dangerous. Emotional explosions can be dangerous, too, when they erupt onto others instead of God's safe arms. But it's not healthy to keep them burning inside, because then the pressure and tension build.

What if you were able to release your emotions to the people in your life in a different way? What if they could come out more like a gentle waterfall than a violent volcano? Beneath each heading below, write out what it might look like in real life for your emotions to come out in these different ways. I've done one example for you.

Violent Volcano	Gentle Waterfall
Yelling	calm voice

> **Give all your worries and cares to God, for he cares about you.**
>
> **1 PETER 5:7 NLT**

How does this verse connect to or support what you've learned about God and your emotions?

 # Pray about it . . .

- Tell God about any emotions you are struggling with right now.

- Ask him to help you release them like a gentle waterfall and give you people in your life who will just listen (not try to fix or correct).

- Admit that you sometimes try to hide your emotions from him and handle them on your own; ask forgiveness for not trusting him to love you in the middle of the explosion.

- Thank God for the way he created your body and mind to grow and change and learn to deal with your emotions.

- Ask him to remind you that they won't always feel this big and explosive.

I'm So Mad, I'm Gonna . . .

Relationships

In your anger do not sin . . .

Ephesians 4:26

"Dude, what is wrong? Why are you so angry?" I asked my twelve-year-old.

"I don't know, Mom. I'm just so mad, and I don't even know why," he replied. And—actually—it made perfect sense.

You see, as your body grows and changes, the hormones inside start messing with things. At the same time your hormone levels are jumping around, the parts of your brain that help you feel emotions are getting stronger, but the part of your brain that helps regulate and react to those emotions isn't developing as quickly. You're left with a body that *feels* more but isn't quite ready to *process* more.

Have you tried walking around in shoes three sizes too big? It's awkward and clumsy and often leads to tripping over your own feet. Right now, the part of your brain that processes emotions is wearing feelings that are three sizes too big for it, which makes everything *feel* like a really big deal.

Feeling big emotions but not understanding them or knowing how to walk in them is hard. God gives us directions for these situations. In Ephesians

4:26, Paul doesn't tell us *not to be angry*; he tells us that our anger should not lead to sin.

It's okay to feel angry. Anger is not a sin, it's a feeling—just like happiness, sadness, or excitement. God created us to feel emotions, but he did not create us to be controlled by them.

Do you see the difference? It's emotion versus action. It's feeling versus doing.

It's okay to feel angry that your mom threw away your math homework not realizing you needed to return it to school. It's not okay to scream, "I hate you!" and stomp off to your room. That's sin—it opposes God's desire for you to honor your parents (see Exodus 20:12).

It's okay to feel angry that your coach didn't name you as a starter on the team; it's not okay to sabotage a teammate or make her look bad so you can get her spot. That's sin—it opposes God's desire for us to live peacefully with one another (see Romans 12:18).

It's okay to feel angry that someone said awful, untrue things about you; it's not okay to spread rumors about her. That's sin—it opposes God's desire for us to love one another, even our enemies (see Matthew 5:44).

The next time you feel that emotion of anger building (and before it trips you up and leads to sin), remind yourself that it's okay to be mad. Give yourself a little grace because your processing brain hasn't caught up to your feeling brain—your shoes are still too big. And then pray this quick prayer: "God, help me not to sin in my anger." Take a deep breath and ask him to show you what to do next.

And, remember, this won't last forever. The processing part of your brain will catch up to the feelings part over the next few years. Your feet will grow, your shoes will fit, and you'll be able to walk through your emotions a little more easily.

Think about it . . .

Some of the time, when we sin in our anger, it's because we haven't given our brains enough time to think through a response; instead, we just react in a sinful way. Make a list of things you could do to release some of the anger when it builds inside you, giving you time to process and then respond instead of react. If you have a plan in mind, you have a better chance of avoiding sin in the middle of anger.

Here are a couple of my favorites: step outside for a breath of fresh air, go for a short walk if I can, write the words, "I am angry because . . ."

You may not express anger outwardly by yelling or in physical ways like punching a wall or hitting a sibling, but that anger is still there. Instead of releasing it, you keep it inside. But you know what? It can be harmful there, too.

Do you ever find yourself nitpicking everything you do, focusing on all the ways you've messed up? Blaming yourself for things that weren't actually your fault? Like that time your friend stopped talking to you for a day and you spent the next week replaying every interaction, trying to figure out what you did wrong. Instead of yelling at her, you beat yourself up about all the things you think you *might* have done wrong.

What do you think Jesus would say to you if he heard all the things you say to yourself inside your head—the blaming, the nitpicking, the anger toward yourself?

> My dear brothers and sisters, take note of this: Everyone should be
> quick to listen, slow to speak and slow to become angry, because
> human anger does not produce the righteousness that God
> desires.
>
> **JAMES 1:19–20**

How does this verse connect to or support what you've learned about emotions and sin?

 Pray about it . . .

- Tell God about the things that make you angry, confess the ways you have sinned in your anger, and ask for forgiveness.

- Thank him for being a loving God, who is slow to anger and who has patience with you.

- Ask God to help you process your emotions well and honor him with your reactions.

Why Do We Have to Feel Pain?

Living

"My thoughts are nothing like your thoughts," says the LORD. "And my ways are far beyond anything you could imagine."

Isaiah 55:8 NLT

The most difficult time to have faith is when we don't understand God's plan. When we are left to feel the emotions of pain and wonder why.

Why do my so-called friends talk about me behind my back?

Why don't I have any friends?

Why are some people just plain mean?

Why can't I be good at sports?

Why can't I get good grades?

Why do school shootings happen?

Why can't someone find a cure for cancer?

Why did my dad lose his job?

Why did my sister, cousin, friend have to die?

Why did I suffer abuse?

Why doesn't my mom love me?

Why did my dad leave?

Why did we have to move?

Why, why, why?

Most of the times I've asked *why*, it's a result of suffering. I rarely ask why after things happen that feel good. It's almost always during times when I feel pain. There's something about pain that makes us feel like we need to understand why. As if knowing the reason something awful happened will somehow make us feel better.

But God did not design us to understand his plans. He did not create us to be equal to him. Sometimes I think God allows us to go through hard things to remind us that he is God and we are not. His thoughts are not like ours. His ways are beyond anything we can understand.

So what are you supposed to do with all those feelings of confusion, anger, disappointment, frustration, sadness, and devastation when things happen and you don't understand why?

I want you to ask a different question. Instead of asking God why this is happening, I want you to ask *yourself* why you can trust God through it.

The Bible isn't just a book we read at church. It's not just a collection of bedtime stories about Jonah and the fish or Moses parting the Red Sea or Jesus walking on water. The Bible is God's Word, and it is full of promises to *you*. It's full of answers to the question *Why can I trust God when bad things happen?*

I can trust God because nothing can separate me from God's love (see Romans 8:37–39).

I can trust God because he promises to work all things for my good— even when I don't understand (see Romans 8:28).

I can trust God because he is with me, he will give me the strength I need to get through this, and he will help me (see Isaiah 41:10).

You can trust God even if you never get the answer to the question *God, why is this happening?* You can feel the peace of God even in the middle of really hard things. But it's not going to happen if you are focused on understanding why bad stuff happens. It can happen if you focus on your good God.

So let's work on shifting your focus, changing your question, and asking God to help you face painful emotions.

 Think about it . . .

When we don't understand why, we can turn to the Bible for reminders about why we can trust God—the promises he has given us. We can also look back at other hard things we've survived to be reminded of how God has helped us. Share one hard thing you have experienced and how God helped you through it.

What *why* questions do you have right now? What hard things are you going through that you don't understand? Or what hard things have you already been through, and you still don't understand why they happened?

This week, instead of giving you another verse to think about connecting to this topic, I want you to look up the verses from the "I can trust God because . . ." statements from this week's devotion and write out the verses. Then write your own "I can trust God because . . ." statement below, with the Bible verse that connects to it.

(If you're struggling to understand a particular *why* right now, consider writing that statement and verse on a note card or making a lock screen out of it so that you can be reminded of why you can trust God through it.)

 Pray about it . . .

- Tell God all the *whys* you struggle with—ask him the hard questions you so badly want to know the answers to.

- Now, give them to him, hand them over, and tell him you no longer need to know why but you *do* need him. (You might want to write these questions on a separate piece of paper, fold them up, and put them in the back of your Bible as a reminder that you've given them to God.)

- Admit that you are not like God and cannot understand everything.

- Ask God to remind you of his promises in the Bible and to help you focus on them instead of trying to figure out why bad things happen.

- Thank God for the ways he's helped you in the past, and ask him to give you the strength to get through the hard things you're experiencing right now.

God's Plan for Love and Dating

I grew up on a farm outside a really small town (remember, I graduated from high school with twenty-eight kids in my class—and we were considered a *big* class). If you drove all the way down the main street from one end of town to the other, you'd pass by the Catholic church and the public school, the post office and bank, a grocery store, and a gas station. You'd drive past Crome's, the grocery store next to the parking lot where high school kids would park their cars next to each other to talk and make plans for how they'd spend their Friday or Saturday night.

And if you kept driving, you'd drive past the elevator and over the river bridge. Like my town, the river was small. On rare occasions, a string of spring storms might cause the current to rush and the water to spill over the banks, but most of the time, the river was low, with sandbars peeking out above the surface.

I used to dream about picnics on those sandbars. I'd picture myself in my boyfriend's car, driving over the bridge, and seeing my name and his drawn in the sand with a heart between. I'd imagine him holding my hand as we waded through the low river current onto the sandbar under the moonlight.

It would all be so perfect. Because that's what love is, right? Perfect?

Over the next few weeks, we're going to explore this idea of love and dating. My prayer is that when we're done, you'll see God—his love and plan for it—more clearly. I pray that your understanding of love would be defined more by God than by Hollywood. And I pray that God prepares your heart for the kind of love he created you to feel and receive.

God's Design for Sex Isn't What the World Has Made It

God

That is why a man leaves his father and mother and is united to his wife, and they become one flesh.

Genesis 2:24

Your world pushes you to grow up a little faster than my world pushed me. At your age, I still might not have known how babies were made. Crazy, right? But you're already seeing messages about sex. It's everywhere—movies, music, shows, even commercials (for the record, I remember ZERO commercials about low testosterone or birth control when I was a kid). You already know more now than I did even a few years past the age you are right now.

I don't want to interrupt your innocence or replace a conversation with your mom or dad, but I want you to hear the biblical message of sex—a message of beauty and love.

Sex is not dirty or wrong. I fear that in being told to wait until marriage, you will unintentionally hear the message that sex is wrong, dirty, or shameful.

It's quite the opposite, actually. God created sex. He designed us for it. "So God created mankind in his own image, in the image of God he created them; male and female he created them" (Genesis 1:27). He created the female body with the male body in mind. We were literally made for each other, to fit together in a perfect, beautiful, and special way. Sex was part of God's plan from the very beginning. When he looked at all his creation—the earth, the oceans, the sky, night and day, plants and animals—and when he looked at the perfect design of man and woman, he was pleased. "God saw all that he had made, and it was very good" (Genesis 1:31).

God designed our bodies for sex, and nothing God creates is dirty or wrong or ugly. God's creation—including sex—is pure, lovely, and beautiful. It is personal and special. Sex as God designed it should be celebrated and respected, not shamed.

Sex is not casual. Our society screams that sex is no big deal, that it's a normal part of romantic relationships. Society tells you that sex doesn't have to mean commitment. Instead, it's simply a way to satisfy physical desires and can be done whenever the urge arises and with whomever. But that is not what God had in mind. The truth is, once you've given yourself to a man, you can never take it back. The memory will always remain, and he will always be a part of your story.

Those moments should be beautiful, treasured, personal memories. Yes, God designed our female bodies to fit perfectly with our male counterparts. But your heart? It was designed for *one* man. I pray even now that God will lead you to the man who cherishes your heart as much as he desires your body.

Sex is not *just* physical. Right now, your view of sex comes only from little glimpses of what you've seen on the screen. You see passion, romance, physical desire, and urgency. But cameras can only record the physical. They cannot capture the emotional and spiritual connection felt in intimate moments between a husband and a wife who were created for each other.

Sex is not simply about satisfying physical desires; it is the ultimate giving of yourself to another. The act of physically surrendering your body to each other is only part of the connection. Intimacy requires trust—revealing yourself physically and emotionally, despite insecurities. It requires a love that reaches far beyond physical attraction. It requires respect and understanding of each other's physical and emotional needs. It requires communication and honesty. The physical surrender on the surface represents a deeper, more intimate surrender of your hearts.

And so, my prayer for you is simple. I pray you find a man who understands your value and loves you as Jesus does, and that, together, you discover the beautiful, intimate kind of marriage and sex God designed you for.

✳ Think about it . . .

Phew. That was a lot, huh? What did you think? (Seriously, write down your reactions to what you've just read.) How do the ideas about God's design for sex differ from the messages you see or hear in your life?

I think you might still have some questions. This is sort of a *big* topic. Write down any questions you have about sex. (You don't have to show them to anyone.)

Now pray over these questions. Ask God to help you understand his design for marriage and sex. Ask him to lead you to people in your life with whom you can talk about sex. And then ask your questions. I know it will be awkward, but it will be worth it. Ask God to give you (and the person you'll talk with) the courage to speak openly. It's important for you to have these conversations now so that your heart is ready when it's time to make decisions about sex and intimacy in the future.

> **Love is patient, love is kind. It does not envy, it does not boast, it is not proud. It does not dishonor others, it is not self-seeking, it is not easily angered, it keeps no record of wrongs.**
>
> **1 CORINTHIANS 13:4–5**

How does this verse connect to or support what you've learned about love and God's design for sex?

Pray about it . . .

- Tell God how you feel about what you've learned this week (scared, freaked out, awkward, shameful, confused, interested, excited).

- Thank him for designing men and women to fit together not just physically but emotionally and spiritually as well.

- Ask God to put people in your life who will help you better understand God's design for marriage and sex.

*I know I already said this, but I just want to say it again. Find someone who loves Jesus and you and whom you trust to talk with about sex and intimacy. Yes, it may be weird, uncomfortable, and awkward, but these conversations are some of the most important you will ever have. You deserve to learn about the most intimate kind of love from people who love you.

**If you've already given your body and a piece of your heart to a boy, you're going to be okay. If you didn't realize that God had a plan for sex before this week, you're going to be okay. God is in the business of creating new hearts for him. He offers mercy, grace, and forgiveness to those who repent and believe. God's design for sex to be pure, lovely, and beautiful has not changed because of anyone's mistake. He loves you and wants you to be loved someday by a man who values your heart and your body. You're going to be okay.

But First, Jesus

Self

> Love the LORD your God with all your heart and with all your soul
> and with all your strength.
>
> Deuteronomy 6:5

Kelsey and Ben sitting in a tree. K-I-S-S-I-N-G. First comes love, then comes marriage, then comes the baby in the baby carriage . . ." So much of life summed up in one fun, teasing, little rhyme.

I don't want to burst anyone's bubble, but love and marriage and parenting aren't quite that simple. But I do think there's some truth in that rhyme . . . first comes love.

It's true. Love comes first. But it's not the love you might immediately think. It's not the romantic kind of love you see in romantic movies or teen romance books. It's not that he-was-my-best-friend-now-he's-my-boyfriend kind of love you might hope for. It's not the high-school-sweethearts kind of love. It's not the Disney princess kind of love.

There's this cheesy line in the '90s movie *Jerry Maguire* when the main character (Tom Cruise) says to the woman he loves, "You complete me." It kind of gives the impression that once you've found the love of your life, you will feel whole, complete.

But that isn't the truth. Human love can't make you feel whole.

The only One who can make you feel whole is Jesus, and that's because his death on the cross made you righteous. He didn't just make you whole; he made you holy in God's sight, restoring your relationship with the God of the universe. His love is unconditional and endless . . . his love never fails.

Human love will fail. At some point, the love of a boy or a man will let you down. You'll feel heartbreak and sadness, disappointment and frustration, unworthiness and loneliness. Don't let someone else's love for you determine your worth. A boy's interest in you makes you no more or less worthy of love. Having a boyfriend doesn't change your value. Even the sweetest and purest human love cannot compare to the love of Jesus, who was willing to die for you.

An imperfect human will never love you perfectly. Only Jesus can do that. Let *him* be your first love.

When you make Jesus your first love, he sets the standard for how you should love and how you should be loved. When you love Jesus first and invite him into relationships with you, he will show you which relationships he approves of and which you need to let go. With Jesus as your first love, you can fight loneliness when dating relationships fall apart, trusting that he remains when others don't.

When Jesus is your first love, real love follows.

✳ Think about it . . .

You might be wondering, *What does it look like to love Jesus first?* Loving Jesus first means making time with him a priority. It means choosing to spend your time with people who honor him in ways that honor him. It means valuing what he says about you more than what people say about you. How does making Jesus your first love impact the way you view dating relationships?

Not only should you make Jesus your first love, but you should expect any boy or man you date to do the same. What things might you notice about a guy who loves Jesus first? What expectations do you have for him?

> ### We love because he first loved us.
>
> **1 JOHN 4:19**

How does this verse connect to or support what you've learned about God's love and making Jesus your first love?

 Pray about it . . .

- Thank God for teaching you what true love means through Jesus.

- Admit that sometimes you fail to love him first, that sometimes you value and desire other people's love more than his.

- Ask God to forgive you for those times and to help you fall more in love with Jesus as you wait to find your *second* love.

Is Prince Charming Out There? And Other Questions about Dating.

Relationships

> Above all, clothe yourselves with love, which binds us all together in perfect harmony.
>
> Colossians 3:14 NLT

This week, I've decided to do things a little differently. I've thought about some common questions about love and dating and done my best to answer them based on what I've learned from experience and the Bible.

IS THERE SUCH A THING AS A PRINCE CHARMING?

Merriam-Webster defines *charm* as "a trait that fascinates, allures, or delights; a physical grace or attraction; compelling attractiveness."[1] The world is full of prince charmings, but I'm not sure that's who you should be looking for. Instead of looking for a guy with charm, look for a guy who displays the fruit of the Spirit: "love, joy, peace, patience, kindness, goodness, faithfulness, gentleness, and self-control" (Galatians 5:22–23 NLT).

DID GOD REALLY CREATE A SPECIFIC MAN JUST FOR ME, TO BE MY HUSBAND?

I don't think God creates humans like pairs of shoes, making a left and a right soulmate. (Please tell me you got that pun—*soul*mate . . . *sole* mate. Sorry. English teacher joke.)

Though the Bible doesn't tell us that God creates our future spouse with us in mind, I do believe that God is sovereign over every detail, including who we will someday marry. God made Eve because it was not good for Adam to be alone. This tells us that God created us for relationships. We also know that God is triune—Father, Son, and Holy Spirit in relationship with each other. Since we are made in God's image, we can recognize that we, too, are made for relationships.

While I can't say for certain that God has created a man with you in mind, I can say that God created you with a need for relationships, and because he loves you and is in control of all things, he will provide for that need.

HOW WILL I KNOW WHO IS THE RIGHT ONE FOR ME?

Pray about it.

Pray about it now.

You're a few years away from having to think about a marriage proposal, but it's never too early to start praying for that moment. Ask God to be clear and lead you to the man he wants you to marry. Ask him to help you avoid anyone who will lead you away from him.

Pray about it then.

When you think you've found *the one*, ask God if he is the one. Ask him for wisdom and insight. And if he says no, ask him to prepare your heart to find the right one.

WHAT IF I PICK THE WRONG ONE AND END UP DIVORCED? WILL GOD HATE ME?

God will not hate you. It is outside his character to hate the people he created. Remember, God *is* love. He is holy and just—*and*, in his love, he provides the gift of grace through the cross.

God does not want any of his children to experience divorce because he knows how devastating and heartbreaking it is. No matter what kind of pain you experience in human relationships, you can be assured that God's love for you never changes.

WHAT IF I NEVER FIND THE RIGHT ONE AND I'M ALONE FOREVER?

Remember how I said that because we are image bearers of God, we have been created to need relationships? And remember how I explained that God has promised to meet the needs he created within us? Marriage isn't the only kind of relationship. A husband isn't the only person who can meet your relationship needs.

Not everyone was created for marriage. Your job is to surrender your desires to God's will and trust in his plan for your life. If marriage isn't part of God's plan for you, you can trust that he will fulfill your relationship needs in other ways, like deep friendships and family. And remember, God has promised never to leave you alone.

 Think about it . . .

Did any of the answers to the questions this week surprise you? Did any of the answers make you want to know more? What questions do you still have about dating and marriage?

Have you made your list yet? The list of all the qualities you want in a future husband? I remember putting these on mine: cute, funny, makes me smile, likes kids, and wears glasses (I know that's a weird one). I'm sure there were a lot more, but those are what I remember. I didn't carry my list around, checking off boxes each time I met a guy, but those characteristics were always in the back of my mind.

What's on your list? Write down the characteristics you'd like to see in a future husband.

I've got a song for you this week again instead of a verse. Listen to "Prince Charming" by Leanna Crawford. How does this song connect to or support what you've learned about dating and marriage?

 # Pray about it . . .

- Tell God all your expectations for your future marriage.

- Ask him to help you have expectations and dreams that align with his plan for your life.

- Thank God for making you in his image with a need for relationships.

- Tell him that you trust him to fill those needs in the way he sees fit because he knows you best.

Why Wait?

Living

> And don't you realize that if a man joins himself to a prostitute, he becomes one body with her? For the Scriptures say, "The two are united into one."
>
> 1 Corinthians 6:16 NLT

Did you read the verse for today? Were you surprised to see the word *prostitute* in a verse from the Bible? I checked several translations, looking for a *tamer* version of that word. I even went to the Greek dictionary to make sure that's what the writer intended. Yep. *Prostitute* is exactly what Paul meant to say.

There's a good chance that when you read "if a man joins himself to a prostitute," you mentally checked out for this week's devotion. After all, you're not a man, and you have no plans to join yourself with a prostitute. While I'm sure that is true, I still think there's value in this verse . . . even for you.

The *Common English Bible* translates this verse, "Don't you know that anyone who is joined to someone who is sleeping around is one body with that person? The scripture says, *The two will become one flesh*" (1 Corinthians 6:16 CEB).

We've already talked about God's design for sex and addressed the fact that it was created to be a pure, beautiful, and lovely experience. But what happens if you grow up a few more years, find *the one* (yes, you remembered to ask God about him), and decide you're ready for that next step because he is *the one* and you know you want to marry him anyway?

The most important part of this verse isn't found in the word *prostitute* or the implication of sleeping around—it's found in the reality that sex unites two people into one. Throughout the Bible, God commands his people not to have sex outside of marriage and to avoid sexual impurity.

God loves you. He wants to protect you from the hurt and pain that happens when sex comes before marriage.

I know this example is way different, but bear with me. Have you ever worn a bandage with superstrength adhesive? The kind you put over a sore, only to create a new one when you tear the bandage off because it rips off the skin around the sore you were protecting. It's almost like that bandage became one flesh with your skin. And tearing it off hurts.

When you join your body with another, you become one flesh. There is deep bonding that happens in that moment, no matter how *casual* the world tells you sex is. A bonding that hurts terribly when pulled apart.

Marriage is a commitment to each other and to God, saying that you intend to remain one flesh for the rest of your earthly lives. No tearing off.

Sweet girl, wait patiently. Wait for a man who will honor God with your relationship. Wait patiently for God's timing. Wait and experience the pure, beautiful, and lovely act of two becoming one flesh in the sweetness of marriage.

PS: All this talk about waiting might make you think, *Why isn't she waiting to tell us about love, sex, intimacy, and marriage?* I know we've covered some really adult topics over the past four weeks. And maybe you didn't feel ready to face some of them. This might be the one area of life that you'd rather remain in childhood than take the step forward into the teenage world. And that's okay. In fact, I think that's better; I wish our world didn't push you so soon. I included this topic not to scare you or gross you out, but because I want you to be prepared. I want you to know these things now so that one day when it's time to make decisions, you'll remember what we've talked about and build your love life on God's love.

 Think about it . . .

I don't like talking about this. I tried to avoid it, but my heart wouldn't let it go. I don't like that you live in a world where you have access to pornography, but the reality is that you do. That doesn't mean you've watched it, but we can't ignore the fact that you could if you wanted to. Or that you could accidentally come across it on a website or video. Or that your friends might try to pressure you into watching it.

The Bible tells us to avoid sexual sin of all kinds. Why might God want you to avoid pornography?

List five married couples you know personally. What do you notice about their relationships that you'd like to see in your own someday? What do you notice that you hope *doesn't* happen in yours?

GOD'S PLAN FOR LOVE AND DATING

> But at the beginning of creation God "made them male and female." "For this reason a man will leave his father and mother and be united to his wife, and the two will become one flesh." So they are no longer two, but one flesh. Therefore what God has joined together, let no one separate.
>
> **MARK 10:6–9**

How does this verse connect to or support what you've learned about waiting for marriage?

 Pray about it . . .

- Tell God what scares you and what excites you about marriage.

- Thank him for the way he loves us and has created us to love and be loved by others as a reflection of his love.

- Admit any sexual sins or desires that you struggle with.

- Ask God to give you the strength to avoid doing anything that doesn't honor his design for intimacy and marriage.

I'm Afraid to Be Myself

Grandma Leta. She was one of the hardest-working, most independent, always-willing-to-help-others, strongest women I've known. Unfortunately, dementia showed up and stole away the woman I had known my whole life and replaced her with an unsure version of herself.

The first time she called me to ask for a recipe, I almost cried. My grandma, who taught me to make cinnamon rolls and ko-laches, needed me to tell her how to make "my" cheese dip, which consisted of dumping Velveeta and Rotel into a crockpot. I remember sitting beside her at a restaurant while the waitress took our orders. She insisted we all order first and then told the waitress she wanted exactly what the person before had ordered. My grandma, who spent decades of her life as a waitress, wasn't able to decide for herself what she wanted to eat, so she just took whatever someone else had decided was good.

That unsure version of herself wasn't who she really was. But I sure can relate to her. Maybe you can too?

Maybe you feel like you're constantly trying to figure out what others want for you and from you. Maybe their expectations make it hard to know what you really want. Maybe you're tired of always doing what others want.

That unsure version of yourself isn't who God wants you to be. God wants you to be who he created you to be, and he wants to use you to love and serve others—not because you have to but because you want to. Over the next four weeks, we're going to explore this idea of expectations and people-pleasing and gain some wisdom about how to combat selfishness with service.

You Don't Have to Please Everyone

God

> But as for me and my household, we will serve the LORD.
>
> Joshua 24:15

Don't forget to finish up your history projects over the weekend. They're a big part of your grade.

Mrs. Taylor

AUNT JULIE

Hey, can you babysit on Saturday?

MOM

I need to run errands on Saturday, want to go along? I'll treat you to ice cream 😄

EM

Sleepover Saturday? Binge Netflix and eat junk food

You love babysitting for Aunt Julie; her kids are so good, and you always have fun. She pays really well, and you're so close to having enough for those

AirPods. But you've been so busy that you haven't been able to do anything with your mom lately, and she's offering to buy ice cream. But you really do need to finish that history project. You still need to do some research, finish the last two slides, and make sure you have all the required pictures. It won't be hard, but you need time to do it. And going to Em's house . . . well, if you don't, she's probably going to be mad, but last time it wasn't that fun, you stayed up too late, and the next day was awful.

No matter what you choose, you're going to let someone down . . . and feel guilty.

I get it. I hate saying no—I never want to disappoint or make anyone mad. I'm forty years old, and I'm just beginning to understand that whole "you can't please everyone" thing. So what do you do? How do you decide who to please and who to let down? And how do you live with the guilt of not being able to make everyone happy?

I think Joshua has the answer.

After Moses died, Joshua led the Israelites as they conquered the land God had promised to them. At the end of Joshua's life, he gave a farewell speech—he warned the people that the nations around them would try to lead them away from God. He knew there would be lots of people and things trying to get their attention. He knew it would be hard. He knew they would have to say no. He knew they couldn't please everyone. He knew they'd have to make a choice.

He didn't tell them what to do, but he told them what *he* was going to do: "But as for me and my household, we will serve the LORD" (Joshua 24:15).

There it is. There's your answer. As for you and your decisions, choose to serve the Lord.

I know this doesn't tell you whether to babysit, run errands with Mom, work on your homework, or go to Em's house, but I do think it can guide you and help you reject the guilt of not being able to please everyone.

You were not created to please people. You were created to serve God. It's okay to say no to people. Many times, the guilt you feel is based on your assumptions about what people will think when you say no and not their feelings at all.

When you are stuck in the middle of people-pleasing and the guilt that follows, ask yourself these things:

1) Will this *not* please God? Is my *no* a result of a sinful attitude? Will a *yes* lead me to sin?

   If you say yes to the sleepover, knowing you'll spend your time talking about other people and listening to music or watching shows that are inappropriate, then that yes leads you to sin.

2) If I say yes, will that choice serve or honor God?

   If you've already committed to babysitting, it honors God to keep your word.

3) Am I letting down a person or am I letting down God?

   Your mom might be disappointed because she loves spending time with you, but you aren't disappointing God.

   If you choose to ignore your homework, you'll let your teacher down, but you'll also let God down because you aren't using the brain, skills, and talents *he* gave you to do the work you need to do.

4) Have I asked God to help me decide what to do?

   God wants to be involved in your decisions, even the little ones. Ask him to help you make choices that serve him and to remove any people-pleasing guilt.

Think about it . . .

Write about a time when you felt the guilt of people-pleasing.

It's hard to say no, especially to good things that just aren't the *right* thing for that moment. Using the scenario from this week's devotion, I want you to practice saying no. Write out a response that you could text or say to Aunt Julie, Mom, and Em as if you were choosing to say no to them. Write each below.

Do not be anxious about anything, but in every situation, by prayer and petition, with thanksgiving, present your requests to God. And the peace of God, which transcends all understanding, will guard your hearts and your minds in Christ Jesus.

PHILIPPIANS 4:6–7

How does this verse connect to or support what you've learned about people-pleasing and saying no?

 Pray about it ...

- Tell God about the struggles you have when it comes to people-pleasing.

- Admit that you have not always made the right choices (ask forgiveness for any that come to mind).

- Ask God to help you make choices that serve him and to help you fight the desire to please people more than him.

- Thank him for loving you and giving you his Word to show you how to live.

You Be ~~You~~ Who God Created You to Be

Self

Do not love this world nor the things it offers you, for when you love the world, you do not have the love of the Father in you. For the world offers only a craving for physical pleasure, a craving for everything we see, and pride in our achievements and possessions. These are not from the Father, but are from this world. And this world is fading away, along with everything that people crave. But anyone who does what pleases God will live forever.

1 John 2:15–17 NLT

The other day, my seven-year-old daughter left the house wearing a bright purple, pink, and blue tie-dyed shirt with mauve floral shorts. I was really tempted to tell her how ridiculous it looked. I considered making her change so that people wouldn't assume she got her fashion sense from me. But—I let her wear it.

I let her wear what she wants now—no matter how unmatched it might be—because, right now, she doesn't care. She doesn't rely on other people's opinions to determine what she wears or likes to do or who she chooses to be. Yet.

That changes, doesn't it? Somewhere over the last few years of your life, you've decided that what other people think is more important than what you think.

So you ask your friends which sports or clubs they're going out for before you make your own choice. You text to see what a friend is wearing to the middle school dance before you pick out your own clothes. You make sure someone else is signed up for camp before giving your parents the permission form. You're never the first to throw out an idea for what to do or where to go or what to eat . . . just in case everyone else thinks it's weird.

Can I tell you something? You don't need someone else's permission to be who you were created to be. God made you with different skills, talents, and interests than your friends. If you like something they don't, it's because you weren't created as clones of each other. Just like your fingertips are unique to you, so are the things you enjoy.

You love playing the saxophone, but none of your friends are going out for band—do it anyway.

All your friends play volleyball or basketball, but you come alive when you're acting—be the only one in your group to audition for the play.

Everyone else wears makeup and follows the latest trends, while you're more comfortable in gym shorts and a T-shirt—wear them anyway.

Been told you may as well use the boys' locker room because you're always playing sports like a guy and fit in better with them? Embrace the female body God gave you *and* the things you love to do.

God did not use one cookie cutter for boys and one cookie cutter for girls and then cut from either pink or blue dough, filling all boys with the same interests and the girls with others.

God didn't use a mold to make you, and you don't have to fit into any that society creates for you. You can be who God created you to be in the body he has given you.

It isn't wrong to want to be liked. It's not sinful to want to connect with people who like the same things you do. But chasing after the approval of other people will wear you out. It's an endless game of tag, and you're always "it." Just as you get close enough to tag someone—to be *cool* enough for them—they step aside and a new standard of *cool* runs by, someone or something else to chase after.

I want you to stop running. Stop chasing. Sit down, right where you are, take a deep breath, and accept that God created you differently from all those other girls running around. And you know what? Those other girls are all chasing someone or something too. When they see you stop running and bravely sit down—boldly being who God created you to be—maybe they'll find the courage to sit down beside you.

 Think about it . . .

In what ways do you feel like you don't fit the mold society or your friend group has created for you? In what ways do you change to try to fit that mold? What is one thing you are hiding because you're worried other people will think it's dumb?

Name one person who has different interests from you, who might feel left out or looked down on because of it. How could you encourage that person to be who God created him or her to be?

In his grace, God has given us different gifts for doing certain things well. So if God has given you the ability to prophesy, speak out with as much faith as God has given you. If your gift is serving others, serve them well. If you are a teacher, teach well. If your gift is to encourage others, be encouraging. If it is giving, give generously. If God has given you leadership ability, take the responsibility seriously. And if you have a gift for showing kindness to others, do it gladly.

ROMANS 12:6–8 NLT

How does this verse connect to or support what you've learned about how God created each of us uniquely?

Pray about it . . .

- Thank God for the gift of being a girl and for the interests and passions he gave you that aren't determined by your gender or your friend group or what anyone else thinks.

- Admit that sometimes it's hard to like things that other people don't.

- Tell God that it's hard to live in a world that says your identity is based on what society tells you instead of who God says you are, and ask him to give you strength and courage to stop chasing after what's cool or popular and to sit bravely as who he created you to be.

- Ask God to help you be who he created you to be in the body he's given you.

- Ask him to help you love, support, and encourage others to be who he created them to be.

You Shouldn't Have to Try Out for Friendships

Relationships

A friend loves at all times, and a brother is born for a difficult time.

Proverbs 17:17 CSB

've already mentioned that I went to a really small school. If I wanted to be on a sports team or in the band or choir or be involved in the play, I didn't have to be *good*, I just had to be breathing. (Seriously, they let anybody in.) Except for cheerleading. There was only so much room on the sidelines for the pom-poms, so they had to limit the number allowed to participate. I remember going to the high school cheerleading interest meeting as an incoming ninth grader with some of my friends. They showed us some cheers, talked about learning a dance routine, went over all the stuff we'd have to buy, and explained how tryouts would be run. It was pretty intimidating.

I imagine all tryouts are like that. I mean, the whole point is to only accept the best, so it makes sense that anyone trying out would have to practice, work hard, and perform at their very best.

You know what you shouldn't have to try out for? Friendships. There shouldn't be auditions. You shouldn't have to practice and play well and meet someone else's standards in order to be called *friend*. You shouldn't be given a friendship grade based on how you measure up to other friends. You shouldn't have to pass a test to get in. Friendship shouldn't be something you earn . . . it should be something you feel.

If a friend expects you to act a certain way, wear a certain thing, or prove your value as a friend, that person isn't really your friend.

A friend loves at all times.

She loves you when you're having a bad day. She loves you when you mess up and ask for forgiveness. She loves you enough to ask for forgiveness when she's messed up. She loves you by caring about what you like and being willing to compromise. A friend notices when you're not quite yourself because she knows who you really are. She doesn't betray your trust. She protects you and knows you'll do the same for her. She doesn't ask you to hide harmful secrets or to treat others in an unloving way. A friend loves at all times, not just when you live up to her standards or only when she needs you.

A friend is born for a difficult time. She listens to your struggles instead of just piling her problems on you. She won't make fun of you when you're hurt by something she doesn't understand. She'll let you share your feelings and ask what she can do. She won't ditch you when someone *better* comes along. She won't avoid you or try to change you in order to make her look better. She won't run away when your life is hard. She'll stand beside you and stand up for you. A friend doesn't disappear when difficulty comes near.

Friendship isn't a competition. There is no spot to be earned or trophy to be given for being the best. Friends are on the same team, working toward the same goal—to make each other better and more like Jesus.

There are plenty of things in this life that you will have to try out for—sports teams, theater or musical groups, jobs, contests—friendship shouldn't be one. In real friendship, you should feel comfortable being who God created you to be. You shouldn't have to try hard or act the part in order to be accepted. Look for friends who love at all times and support you through difficult times. These are the friendships that last.

 # Think about it . . .

Think about your closest friends. Write their names below. How do you feel when you're around them? Do you enjoy spending time with them, or does it feel like work? Are you comfortable with them, or do you feel like you're constantly trying to meet expectations? Do you look forward to seeing them, or do you feel nervous or anxious? Are the friends on your list friends who love at all times? Are they friends who support you through difficult times?

You were created for friendship (remember, God said it wasn't good for Adam to be alone), and if you haven't found your real friends yet, it can feel really lonely.

I believe that God has friendship—good friendship—planned for you, even if you haven't found it yet. I believe he is preparing friendship for you right now. He's preparing a friend who will love, support, encourage, and endure with you.

If you haven't found this friend yet, pray for her. Pray that God would show her to you. He has already planned your meeting and the growth of your friendship. Write a prayer for her below. Tell God what you want and need and ask him to provide.

Dear God, bring me a friend who . . .

> **Therefore encourage one another and build each other up, just as in fact you are doing.**
>
> **1 THESSALONIANS 5:11**

How does this verse connect to or support what you've learned about friendship this week?

 Pray about it . . .

- Thank God for creating you for friendship and for promising to put people in your life to love and support you well.

- Tell God about your friendships.

- Thank him for the friends you have who treat you well and accept you as you are.

- Ask God to help you see any unhealthy friendships and to show you how to make them better or to walk away from them in a loving way.

- Ask him to send you good friends and to help you be one.

A Selfie Doesn't Show Everything

Living

Don't be selfish; don't try to impress others. Be humble, thinking of others as better than yourselves. Don't look out only for your own interests, but take an interest in others, too.

Philippians 2:3–4 NLT

We've talked a lot lately about being who God made you to be and that your first focus should be on pleasing God, not necessarily pleasing people. We talked about how he created you with specific interests and talents and how you can embrace those and stop chasing what other people think you should be or do. We've talked about how real friends shouldn't require you to change to be a part of their team. Basically, we've talked a lot about you. So I can see how you might begin to think that the world revolves around you.

Actually, *your* world does revolve around you, and there is *so* much going on inside of it right now that it's really easy to forget that anything or anyone exists outside. Some of that is natural for the phase of life you're in, and some of that has been influenced by the way our world is.

Imagine ten phones laid out on a table in front of you, belonging to different groups of people. Some belong to parents, others to grandparents, some to middle school girls, some to teen boys. You get ten seconds with the phone's camera roll to identify which group each phone belongs to. Who do you think the phones with the most selfies belong to? My guess is middle or high school girls.

You live in a selfie kind of world—it's how people document and share their lives. Unfortunately, that mentality sometimes drifts over into the way we see (or don't see) other people. Your world is full of selfies.

Upset with your mom for making another meal you don't like, you comment about how awful it is. That selfie view doesn't show her at the store earlier that day putting back a package of her favorite snack so she could make sure there was room in the budget to fill your lunch box for the track meet.

You storm into the house after finding your bike chain still hanging from the gears, even though your dad said he'd have it fixed for you so you could ride it to your friend's house. That selfie view doesn't show how tired he was when he walked into the house from work and went straight to the dishwasher to help your mom unload it.

After checking your grades online to see if your math test has been graded, you text a friend to complain about how your teacher never gets things graded. That selfie view doesn't show your teacher sitting on his couch grading papers at 11:00 p.m. after his own kids are in bed.

Annoyed with your classmate, who was supposed to work on her part of the group project last night but showed up at school without anything done, you roll your eyes and whisper a comment to your friend. That selfie view doesn't show your classmate helping her little brother with his homework, making supper, and then putting him to bed because their mom was working late.

The problem with selfies is that they don't show everything. If you're the only one in the photo, you don't see everything happening around you. You don't see the people outside your small screen.

God didn't create you for selfies. He created you to be selfless. I want you to become who God created you to be, which is a young woman who sees and loves others. Sometimes that means switching the camera out of selfie mode and looking through a wider lens.

 Think about it . . .

So maybe you don't take selfies that often, or maybe you don't even have a phone, but can you think of a time when you had a selfie kind of attitude? Write about it here, and consider what your selfie didn't show.

In this week's verse, Paul tells us to take an interest in others too. What could you do this week to take an interest in someone else (your friends or classmates, your family members, your teachers or coaches)? Write some ideas below, and circle at least one to follow through on. Come back once you've done it, and write about their reaction and how it made you feel.

> Offer hospitality to one another without grumbling. Each of you should use whatever gift you have received to serve others, as faithful stewards of God's grace in its various forms.
>
> **1 PETER 4:9–10**

How does this verse connect to or support what you've learned about a selfie attitude?

 Pray about it . . .

- Admit to God that you sometimes choose to be selfish over being selfless, and ask for forgiveness for specific situations.

- Ask him to help you be a more selfless person and to remind you to look for ways to serve others.

- Thank God that he always forgives you and never gives up on you no matter how many times you mess up.

Surviving a Changing World with an Unchanging God

Booyah. Fo Shizzle. Talk to the hand. Holla.

These words existed when I was your age but would sound like an awkward foreign language coming from your lips.

There are words in *your* vocabulary that didn't even exist when I was your age. I bet you can come up with a few—think about the words that hearing your parents say in public would make you cringe.

The words we use change from year to year, generation to generation. That's why it feels like you need a dictionary when you read the classics like *The Outsiders*, "The Tell-Tale Heart," *The Adventures of Tom Sawyer*, "The Gift of the Magi," or *The Secret Garden* in your language arts class.

Speaking of the dictionary, did you know that hundreds of new entries are added each year? Words that didn't exist before but have been so commonly used in recent years that they earned their spot in the English language forevermore. Words like *dumbphone*, *laggy*, *yeet*, *sus*, *ICYMI*, and *level up*.

Language, like everything in our world, is constantly changing. You, as a middle school girl, might be the one to feel that change the most—changes in your body, your emotions, your hormones, your responsibility, your friendships, your brain, your interests. It feels like *everything* is changing. And it sort of is.

Change is a part of your life, but it doesn't have to change who you are. In the next four weeks, we'll take a look at all those changes and how your faith can keep you focused through them.

I Am Changing, Jesus Is Not

God

Jesus Christ is the same yesterday and today and forever.

Hebrews 13:8

Your body is going through some major physical changes, isn't it? Some changes only you notice, but there are some that others can very much see. It's such a weird place to be. On one hand, it's exciting to think about becoming and looking more like a woman. On the other, it's terrifying.

These changes don't happen overnight. It's not like you wake up one morning three inches taller with a C-cup and curvy hips. Instead, you notice hair where it wasn't before, zits popping up (okay, that one happens overnight), and a need for a sports bra in gym class rather than wearing one just because everyone else has one.

With your body (brain and emotions and hormonal system) going through so much change, it's easy to feel overwhelmed by it all. It feels like you aren't the same person today as you were yesterday. And who knows who you'll be tomorrow?

Your world is going through some major changes too. On top of all the stuff happening internally, you're experiencing change all around you. Changing schools. Changing friends. Changing interests. Changing teachers. Changing classes. Changing style. Very few things in your life feel the same as they did just a couple years ago. As soon as you feel steady, something else shifts in your life.

I wish I could tell you when puberty ends and the full change to woman has happened that your changing years would be over. But that's not true. The truth is, you will continue to experience change in every phase of life—some changes will be good and necessary, others hard and painful. Each change will present the chance to grow into the woman God has created you to be and to strengthen your faith.

Here's what I want you to remember every time you encounter change: Jesus understands the confusion and difficulty of human changes, yet his mission in life never changed. He came to this earth to save sinners. He lived on this earth to save sinners. And he died on this earth to save sinners.

Think about this . . . Jesus went through puberty. It's kind of weird to think of Jesus as a thirteen-year-old boy, isn't it? His body physically changed in the same way your male classmates' bodies change—his voice cracked and facial hair appeared. He endured the hormone shifts and physical changes to his body, similar to your own.

But here's the crazy thing—even though Jesus endured the physical changes of puberty, his mission didn't change and neither did his character. He is the same yesterday, today, and forever.

Jesus is holy and without sin. Jesus is loving, compassionate, and patient. Jesus doesn't ignore sin, but he does offer grace, mercy, and forgiveness. Jesus is obedient to God the Father and does the work God has planned for him. He is all these things, all the time.

When you begin to get overwhelmed by all the changes going on in your body and your world, consider your own mission in life: to love God and others. Despite everything changing within you and outside you, that mission remains. Jesus remains too. Just as he walked the dusty roads of Nazareth as a thirteen-year-old boy with grace, patience, and mercy, he walks this road to adulthood with you in the same way. He will never leave you, and he will always love you—no matter what else changes.

 **Think about it . . .**

What physical changes are you dealing with right now? List out all the things that seem to be different about you today compared to a month ago. Or maybe you're feeling desperate for these changes to begin. It seems like you're way behind in the becoming-a-woman race, and you're tired of running. If that's the case, list out all the things you're expecting to change in the next year. Circle things that you're excited about and underline things that scare you a little.

How does it make you feel knowing that Jesus never changes? Go back to this week's devotion and underline the characteristics of Jesus that never change. In this space, write down your answers to the following: Which are you most grateful for and why? Which do you need to be reminded of and why?

> Long ago you laid the foundation of the earth
> and made the heavens with your hands.
> They will perish, but you remain forever;
> they will wear out like old clothing.

> **You will change them like a garment**
> **and discard them.**
> **But you are always the same;**
> **you will live forever.**
>
> **PSALM 102:25–27 NLT**

How does this verse connect to or support what you've learned about God this week?

 Pray about it . . .

- Tell God about the changes you are going through and how you feel about them.

- Thank him for creating your body in such a remarkable way that your body and your brain and your hormones all change together, moving you toward becoming an adult.

- Admit that these changes are hard and sometimes you feel like it's out of your control.

- Ask God to remind you that Jesus never changes and that you can always rely on the steadiness of God no matter what changes you go through.

Who Am I Supposed to Be?

Self

> This means that anyone who belongs to Christ has become a new person. The old life is gone; a new life has begun!
>
> 2 Corinthians 5:17 NLT

Name three things you liked a year ago that you don't like today (think foods, music, shows, activities, etc.). Write them in the margin. Name three things you've outgrown in the past year (clothes, shoes, hairstyle, etc.). Write those in the margin too. If you compared a picture of yourself from fourth grade to a picture of you right now, would you look the same?

You've changed, haven't you? In the past couple years, a lot has changed about you. The things you like, the way you look—the person you are has changed. Those changes can make you feel like you are a little lost: like you don't quite remember who you were, you're not exactly sure who you are now, and you don't really know who you want to become.

I'm sure you've been asked about what you want to be when you grow up. It feels like you only have six to eight years—middle school and high school—to figure out who you are and who you want to be. It can feel like the next five *years* of your life determine who you're supposed to be for the next five *decades*. That's a lot of pressure.

What classes should I take in high school? Should I get a summer job? Does that need to match up with what I want to do someday? How do I spend the money I make? What career path should I take, and do the classes I take now need to match that? What if I change my mind?

Listen, all those things are important, and I'm proud of you for thinking about them. But they don't determine who you are.

Yes, there will be a lot of change in the next few years. Yes, you'll feel like you're turning into someone very different from who you were in those pictures your mom likes to keep on her phone. Yes, you will make some mistakes.

But I want you to remember who God says you are. The Bible says you are a new person when you put your faith in Jesus as your personal Savior—a new person made to become more like him every day.

This doesn't mean you'll believe in Jesus and wake up perfect the next morning. The urge to talk back to your parents or yell at your sibling won't suddenly disappear. You won't wake up longing to read your Bible and pray all day long. You won't wake up with an intense desire to be kind to that one girl in your class who makes you crazy.

Salvation doesn't instantly make you a new, perfect person. It makes you a new person who wants to be like Jesus and who recognizes when she isn't. Her old life of chasing after what feels good in the moment is fading, and her new life of wanting to do things that honor God is beginning.

That change—that new person—isn't completely dependent on you. It's possible because the power of Jesus lives inside you through the Holy Spirit. *He* is making you a new person.

A summer job or career path doesn't change that. The classes you take in high school or the activities you choose to participate in don't change that. The amount of money you make or the clothes you wear don't change that. You are a new person because Jesus died on the cross for you. And that changes everything.

 Think about it . . .

In what ways do you feel the pressure that the decisions you make now will impact who you will become in the future?

How does realizing that you are a new person in Jesus relieve that pressure? Does it add to it in any way?

> Once you were dead because of your disobedience and your many sins. You used to live in sin, just like the rest of the world, obeying the devil—the commander of the powers in the unseen world. He is the spirit at work in the hearts of those who refuse to obey God. All of us used to live that way, following the passionate desires and inclinations of our sinful nature. By our very nature we were subject to God's anger, just like everyone else.
>
> But God is so rich in mercy, and he loved us so much, that even though we were dead because of our sins, he gave us life when he

> raised Christ from the dead. (It is only by God's grace that you have
> been saved!)
>
> EPHESIANS 2:1–5 NLT

How does this verse connect to or support what you've learned about being
a new person in Jesus?

 Pray about it . . .

- Tell God about all the pressure you feel when it comes to who you will
  become.

- Thank him for saving you and being the power behind the new person
  you are becoming through salvation.

- Admit that even though you believe in Jesus, fighting sin is still hard.
  Confess the sins you are struggling with.

- Ask God to help you become more like Jesus every day.

Not All Friends Are Forever

Relationships

All people are like grass,
    and all their faithfulness is like the flowers of the field.
The grass withers and the flowers fall,
    because the breath of the LORD blows on them.
    Surely the people are grass.
The grass withers and the flowers fall,
    but the word of our God endures forever.

Isaiah 40:6–8

In my friends' high school yearbooks next to my signature, I wrote things like *BFF, friends forever, I'll never forget you, we have to make sure we hang out, we'll always be friends* . . .

Aside from the two class reunions I've been to and a few weddings in the last twenty years, I haven't spent quality time with most of the people I wrote those words to.

That doesn't mean they weren't important to me. It doesn't mean I've completely forgotten them (I text a few occasionally). It doesn't mean I no longer like them or have pushed them out of my life.

It means that friendships change. And that's okay.

Friendships can change because you change. Or because people move away. Or because interests change and the things you used to do together become things you no longer do at all. They change because of deep hurt and the destruction of trust. Or because you outgrow them or have different needs. Regardless of the reason, not all friends are forever. And that's hard.

Here are some things to consider when a friendship ends.

Not all friendships honor God. God wants you to grow in your faith, so you need to surround yourself with people who will grow beside you. Sometimes that means the weeds must be pulled. Friendships that lead you toward ungodly things are weeds. Friendships that compete with God, sucking up all your time and energy, are weeds. Unhealthy friendships that make you feel unworthy and inadequate are weeds. Maybe the loss of a friendship is God pulling the weeds from your life so that you can grow closer to him.

Maybe those friendships are seasonal. A sunflower stalk grows tall and strong, producing big, bright, yellow flowers. Though they are strong enough to withstand the Midwest weather, including hail, high winds, tornadoes, and sometimes drought, they can't grow forever. When the cold Kansas winter hits, the sunflowers die, leaving the field empty, waiting for spring to come and new planting to begin. Some friends are like that—strong and bright, withstanding some tough storms, yet not meant to bloom forever. Some friendships need to end so that new friendships can begin.

No matter how many friendships you go through or how many times they change, remember (again) that God never changes. His Word lives forever, and his Word says this:

1. You've been created for friendship—remember God didn't want Adam to be alone (see Genesis 2:18).
2. God delights in giving you good gifts (Matthew 7:11), and I think that includes friendship. God wants to see you feel loved (John 13:34).

If a friendship has ended, you can trust that God sees the reason behind it even though you can't. Tell him how badly it hurts. Feel the disappointment. And trust that, even though you can't see it, he's building a friendship that honors him and fills the needs he knows you'll have.

 Think about it . . .

List out all the friendships you remember having—current and past—in the middle of the space below (leave room to write beside them and below them). Next to each, on the right, write down one thing you love(d) about it. Is there anything about those friendships that feels/felt off? If so, write about it below the friendship. Circle any friendships that haven't lasted or might not last forever. Write why in the left margin.

Since we've been talking about weeds and flowers, I've got an activity for you today. Look below at the two flower beds. Notice the one on the right. It looks well-kept, and the flowers are strong and beautiful. The one on the left looks a little run-down; it's full of weeds, and it's obvious that the flowers suffer because of it. In the box on the right, write down the qualities you want to see in your friends or things you want them to do. In the box on the left, write qualities that good friends wouldn't show or things they wouldn't do. When you're done, feel free to color the friendship gardens.

The LORD is close to the brokenhearted; he rescues those whose spirits are crushed.

PSALM 34:18 NLT

How does this verse connect to or support what you've learned about friendship?

Pray about it . . .

- Tell God about your friendships—the good stuff and the hard stuff.

- Thank him for sending you friends, even if only for a season, and for promising to plant new friendships when old ones fade away.

- Admit if sometimes you feel lonely and struggle to trust that God has good friends planned for you.

- Ask God to help you find and grow friendships that honor him and fill you up.

Change Scares Me

Living

In my distress I called to the LORD; I cried to my God for help. From his temple he heard my voice; my cry came before him, into his ears.

Psalm 18:6

One of the clearest memories of my wedding day is standing next to my little sister outside the reception. Her hands were wrapped around my waist in a sort of side hug. And she was crying. While I consoled and said goodbye to my sister (who I would see the next morning), my new husband waited patiently in my brother's car (both of ours were out of sight to avoid the traditional "decorating" with shaving cream and aluminum cans).

It wasn't the first time my ten-year-old sister cried about me getting married. Though she loved Ben (my husband), she did not love the idea of him taking me away from her. Her world was changing. Her big sister would no longer spend summers at home. Her big sister would no longer be around to braid her hair before a softball game or to walk with her around the fairgrounds. Her relationship with her big sister was changing.

Change is scary because it means accepting the fact that you don't know what will happen next. Fear and anxiety scream what-ifs into your brain. The fear and anxiety make you feel alone, wondering how you'll survive the un-known of what's ahead. The what-if thoughts change into *I can't do this*.

Those thoughts bounce around like Ping-Pong balls. Ping, ping, ping. The noise makes it impossible to hear anything else—especially the quiet whisper of God's voice, assuring you that he sees your fear and hears your cries.

I wish my little sister were here today. This is what I would tell her about change . . .

When the unknown of change feels scary and the what-ifs won't stop bouncing, remember these four things:

1) God knows all things. He doesn't wonder what if, he knows what will be. "Before a word is on my tongue you, Lord, know it completely" (Psalm 139:4).

2) God loves me so much that he sent his Son to die for me. If he loves me that much, I can trust he's going to make sure I'm okay. "For God so loved the world that he gave his one and only Son, that whoever believes in him shall not perish but have eternal life" (John 3:16).

3) God has protected me through hard things before, and he is with me now—he is my help and shield. "We wait in hope for the Lord; he is our help and our shield. In him our hearts rejoice, for we trust in his holy name. May your unfailing love be with us, Lord, even as we put our hope in you" (Psalm 33:20–22).

4) God is always with me. When change makes me feel weak and afraid, God can fill me with his strength and courage. "Have I not commanded you? Be strong and courageous. Do not be afraid; do not be discouraged, for the Lord your God will be with you wherever you go" (Joshua 1:9).

See the back of the book for a cutout you can keep to remember these things.

Think about it . . .

What is the biggest example of change you can think of in your life? During that time, who or what helped you get through it? What role do you think God had in helping you—putting people in your life or working in the situation?

What changes are happening in your life now or in the near future? What scares you about those changes?

Choose one of the verses from the four things to remember when change is scary and explain how it can help you face change.

 # Pray about it . . .

- Tell God about the things that scare you about change.

- Tell him how amazing it is that he already knows what will happen. Thank him for loving you, for helping you through past changes, and for promising to be with you through future changes.

- Admit any changes that you are struggling to deal with.

- Ask God to help you handle change well, not just right now but future changes too.

Boundary Isn't a Bad Word

My thirteen-year-old and ten-year-old wanted to buy a pair of Orbeez guns. They "would give them something to do" over the summer. They promised to wear eye gear when they played with them. They assured us the little ball-bullets wouldn't make a mess or break anything. They had their own money saved up and ready to spend.

Their dad and I said no. Not because we're fun suckers (though I usually am), but because we were thinking of all the things they weren't.

We were thinking about their one-year-old brother trying to eat the squishy little balls. We were thinking about their

three-year-old brother getting ahold of one and shooting himself . . . or the neighbor's cats. We were thinking about the po-
tential for things to break and then the devastation of being
plunged back into boredom after having them taken away. We
were thinking about how these toys would be fun for about a
week and then find themselves lying in the garage or basement,
unused (much like the laser tag guns or the hoverboard or the
countless other not-cool-anymore toys we have).

We said no because we saw more.

Sometimes God says no to us too. Because he sees more.
These nos—these boundaries—they're not all bad. In fact, they're
for our good. *Boundary* isn't a bad word, and over the next four
weeks, we're going to discover why.

God Tells the Ocean Waves Where to Stop

God

Who kept the sea inside its boundaries as it burst from the womb, and as I clothed it with clouds and wrapped it in thick darkness? For I locked it behind barred gates, limiting its shores.

I said, "This far and no farther will you come. Here your proud waves must stop!"

Job 38:8–11 NLT

The wet sand felt cool beneath my bare feet. The waves gently rolled over my toes and then withdrew back into the ocean, my feet just slightly deeper in the sand than before. I took a deep breath and felt the water hit my feet again. I had never experienced anything like it before.

I was familiar with the creek just east of my house, where my brothers, cousins, and I searched for frogs. The water there was usually quiet, barely trickling within the banks. I had seen the river just outside town swell with rainwater as the current raged and spilled over the banks that normally held it in. The floodwater sat motionless for a few days before the ground absorbed all it needed and the current carried the excess downriver. Before long, the river was back within its banks—where it belonged.

But the ocean . . . the ocean had no banks to contain its saltwater. There was no dam or cliff to stop the flow. Only a sandy beach where the water spread wide along the shore and then returned to the sea. Compelled by *something* on the beach—though nothing I could see—to simply stop, turn around, and flow back to where it came from.

I couldn't see the boundary that kept the water from flowing farther onto the beach, but it was there. It wasn't made by humans—it wasn't a physical form of dirt or rock . . . it was the hand of God.

There are over 95,000 miles of shoreline in the United States.[1] Miles and miles of ocean water rolling over and up to beaches, rocky shores, and cliffs. God's hands stretch across 95,000 miles as a barrier between sea and land.

God set the boundary between ocean and land. That's how awesome he is. That's how powerful he is. That's how attentive, wise, and intentional he is. The ocean doesn't just flow wherever it wants; it flows only where God has decided to allow it.

Can you just think about that for a minute? Just sit and think about how amazing it is that ocean waves flow over the sand and then simply and gently return to the sea. Now, look back at our verse for this week, especially the last line, where God says to the ocean waters, "This far and no farther will you come" (Job 38:11). I imagine God standing along the shoreline, speaking these words in a calm yet strong and firm voice. He's not screaming at the waves because they've been unruly. There isn't distrust in his voice, as if he expects them to get out of line and wreak havoc. He simply shares his expectations and makes it clear that they will follow them. God—in all his power and might—sets a boundary for the waves with a gentle and loving voice that reminds them their creator knows what's best. *Boundary* isn't a bad word; it's an act of love.

 Think about it . . .

Have you ever seen the ocean? What do you know or remember about it?
If you've never been there yourself, find a video online of the waves on an
ocean beach. During stressful times, people often say they need a trip to the
beach. Beaches around the world attract millions of visitors each year. Why
do you think people love spending time at the beach?

In your own words, define the word *boundary*. Is a boundary a good or a bad
thing? How does your view of boundaries connect to the idea that God set
the boundary for the ocean?

> This is what the LORD says, he who appoints the sun to shine by
> day, who decrees the moon and stars to shine by night, who stirs
> up the sea so that its waves roar—the LORD Almighty is his name . . .
>
> JEREMIAH 31:35

How does this verse connect to or support what you've learned about God's
power and might and the way he sets boundaries?

 ## Pray about it . . .

- Tell God how amazing he is.

- Thank him for caring about you—the same God who stops the ocean waves sent Jesus to die on the cross . . . for *you*.

- Admit that sometimes you forget how big and magnificent God is.

- Ask God to help you know him better.

Psst . . . You Don't Have to Be Involved in Everything

Self

By the seventh day God had finished the work he had been doing;
so on the seventh day he rested from all his work.

Genesis 2:2

Volleyball (manager), basketball (player and manager), FCCLA, FFA, NHS, choir, band, scholar's bowl, drama, forensics/speech, summer softball, 4-H, waitress—all the things I listed under activities when filling out college scholarship applications. I had come to the conclusion that the longer the list, the better you looked. So I did it all.

There are more options available to make that list even longer today: travel sports, club teams, countless school clubs, community groups, sports camps, drama/music/art camps, special programs that require applications and approval to be a part of, and on and on and on.

You live in a world with endless opportunities for ways to get involved. And over the next few years, you're going to hear that a lot. *Get involved. Try something new. Go out for everything and figure out what you like. If you're bored or lonely, it's because you aren't in enough sports or clubs or groups or activities. Do it all.*

The opportunities for involvement and activities may be endless, but the amount of time and energy you have is not. You cannot do it all.

Remember, God created day and night, right? He gave us twenty-four hours in each day, knowing that we would need some of that time to eat and sleep. If it feels like the time we have each day is not enough to do it all, we might be doing things God didn't create us to do. We might be doing more than he expects us to.

Here's the truth about that activities list on scholarship applications: the longer it is, the more tired you are.

Sure, it's possible to go from a before-school club meeting to eight hours of school to sports practice to a babysitting job to working on a 4-H project to finishing homework to bed. You can squeeze a million things into the day, moving from one activity to the next, adding things to your activities résumé, but you know what you'll be missing? Rest.

Not the eight-to-nine-hours-of-sleep kind of rest (though that's really important too), but the kind of rest that gives you permission to just exist and not *do* all the time. The kind of rest that God created you to need. The kind of rest God enjoyed after creating the world.

I know you don't always like to hear this, but you're still a kid. And it's okay to act like one. It's okay to enjoy this time in your life when you don't *have* to be busy. It's okay to come home from school and draw or color or read or play outside without working toward any end goal. That's a form of rest.

There are so many good things to be involved in (sports and clubs, part-time jobs, and after-school activities), but you cannot get the good from them if you don't have time to enjoy them. If you feel rushed from one thing to the next, doing just to do, that might mean you're doing too much. It's okay to tell your parents or friends that you don't want to join that club or play that sport.

Here's my advice: do what you love, and leave time for rest.

 **Think about it . . .**

List out all the activities you are involved in. Circle the ones you *love*, the ones you'd drive hours to do and not complain once. Underline the ones you do mostly because someone else has told you to (your parents encouraged you to try it, a friend wanted someone to do it with, an older sibling did it so now you do). Cross out any that you show up to but don't really enjoy that much.

Consider talking about your list with your parents, especially if you've underlined or crossed any activities off.

What would it look like for you to enjoy rest? If you had one hour you didn't *have* to be anywhere or *do* anything, how would you spend it? When was the last time you enjoyed rest? How is rest a type of boundary?

> For all who have entered into God's rest have rested from their labors, just as God did after creating the world. So let us do our best to enter that rest. But if we disobey God, as the people of Israel did, we will fall.
>
> **HEBREWS 4:10–11 NLT**

How does this verse connect to or support what you've learned about rest?

 Pray about it ...

- Thank God for creating you with a need for rest, that you're not just some robot with a lifelong battery.

- Tell God about the activities you are in, any pressure you feel to be involved, and any nervousness you feel about choosing activities over the next couple of years.

- Ask God to help you make wise decisions about what to be involved in and what to say no to.

- Admit that stopping for rest is hard when our society teaches that busy is better, and ask God to show you how to rest and how to make it a priority.

My Parents Don't Let Me Do Anything

Relationships

Honor your father and your mother, as the LORD your God has commanded you, so that you may live long and that it may go well with you in the land the LORD your God is giving you.

Deuteronomy 5:16

You know what a rumble strip is, right? The grooves in the asphalt just on the other side of the white lines on the edge of a highway with the purpose of warning and protecting drivers.

Imagine a sleepy driver, eyelids heavy, head nodding as she dozes off, just for a split second. The car veers over the white line, a line she can't see because her eyelids have fallen shut. But the noise of the rumble strips? That she hears. Her eyes pop open, and she shakes her head quickly as she guides the car back within the safety of the lines. (And hopefully she pulls over to rest or walk around or do something to get her brain and body ready to drive again.)

Now, if you're a passenger trying to take a nap in the car, the noise of a rumble strip is more annoying than anything else. But someday, when you're the driver, you'll appreciate the way they warn and protect you.

Kind of like the boundaries your parents set for you.

I know sometimes it feels like your parents make rules and set boundaries just to annoy you, to keep you from doing the fun stuff your friends are doing.

Technology and social media limits. Curfews. Restrictions and filters on the internet or your phone (if you have one). Limits to the number of fun activities you get to do. Rules about snacks and mealtimes and limits on junk food and energy drinks.

Sometimes it feels like your parents set boundaries for *everything*, but the truth is, they're doing everything they can to warn and protect you because you mean everything to them. They're building a road for you and placing rumble strips along each side. They aren't putting them down to torture you or make you miserable. They're putting them there to protect you because they know the danger that lies outside them. Right now, you're still a passenger in the car, annoyed by the noise. But your parents are preparing you (in so many ways) to be the one in the driver's seat. The boundaries they set today are getting you ready for tomorrow.

Can I tell you something else about your parents and those rumble strips? They didn't grow up driving the same highway you're on now. The rumble strips their parents set up for them won't work for you because the road looks so much different from how it did when they were the passengers. They don't always know what they're doing, but I promise they're doing it all out of love.

Give them some grace, would you? Calmly talk to them when you feel like the rumble strips are on the wrong side of the white line and don't give you enough space to drive. And, every once in a while, maybe even thank them for warning and protecting you, even if you don't like the noise their rumble strips make.

 Think about it . . .

Which boundaries set by your parents annoy you the most? What might those rumble strips be warning you about or protecting you from? What could you do to show that you're ready for a little more space on the road? What do you wish your parents understood about how you feel about those boundaries?

Parents are told that kids actually *want* boundaries. Is that true? Why or why not? Even if you feel like you don't want boundaries, how is respecting their boundaries a way of honoring your parents?

> **Children, obey your parents in everything, for this pleases the Lord.**
>
> **COLOSSIANS 3:20**

How does this verse connect to or support what you've learned about boundaries and your relationship with your parents?

 *Pray about it ...*

- Tell God about the boundaries you are struggling with.

- Ask him to show you whether you're struggling with them because your rebellious, sinful nature just wants to do what you want or if you've actually outgrown them and are ready for more freedom.

- Thank God for parents who love you and are trying their best.

- Ask God to open your heart to accepting boundaries and to guide any conversations with your parents about them.

Sometimes, You Need to Unplug

Living

Yet the news about him spread all the more, so that crowds of people came to hear him and to be healed of their sicknesses. But Jesus often withdrew to lonely places and prayed.

Luke 5:15–16

Can you imagine Jesus carrying around an iPhone? The notifications would be *constant*. Text messages asking for advice. Live location Snapchats of broken bones, sent in hopes Jesus would swing by and do a quick healing miracle. Videos of the Pharisees trashing him, filmed by passersby who thought Jesus should see what they were saying behind his back.

Ping. Ping. Ping. I can hear the constant stream of notifications.

I wonder what Jesus would have done with an iPhone.

Actually, I think I know. He would have unplugged. Shut it down. Turned it off.

He didn't have a smartphone, but that's sort of what he did anyway. When the demands for healing and teaching and miracles got intense, Jesus withdrew. He went to lonely places and prayed. He walked away from the constant needs and rested with God his father. Remember how we talked a couple weeks ago about your God-created need for rest? Even Jesus set boundaries to protect his rest.

Maybe you need to do that too? I mean, if it worked for Jesus, I think it will work for you.

The ability to connect with friends 24/7 can be a really great thing. If you need help on homework or are feeling lonely or need someone to talk to, it's nice to know your friends are just a message away. But the 24/7 connection can also be draining. When a friend sends a message, the urge to respond *instantly* is strong. Strong enough to make you ignore or forget about everything else around you. If you send a friend or classmate a message without an immediate response, the what-ifs in your brain begin to form. *What if they're mad at me? What if they're ignoring me? What if I said something stupid?* This constant connection can lead to constant anxiety.

Social media adds another complicated layer to this idea of connection. Sure, it's fun to post pictures and see those that others share. Social media apps allow you to connect with friends from other towns or schools, but the comparison social media creates can be a really awful thing. Seeing your friends hanging out together without you hurts. Being constantly aware of what everyone else is doing is overwhelming. Trying to *earn* likes and comments is draining. It's easy to get sucked into the mindless scrolling that traps you into the just-one-more-video mindset until suddenly you look up from your phone and realize an hour has passed.

Smartphones and social media can be demanding and exhausting. And you need a break.

Set boundaries with technology and your phone. Unplug. Shut it down. Turn it off. Do not allow your phone to have 24/7 access to your brain or your heart. Jesus is *God*, and even he stepped away. You can too.

Maybe you don't have a phone yet, but in our world, it seems nearly impossible to make it through life without one, so it's likely in your future. Maybe your parents set limits and boundaries on the way you use your phone now, but one day it's going to be your job. Be ready to spend time with it wisely.

 # Think about it . . .

Could you survive a day without a device? A week? A month? What would be the hardest part of living without instant connection to friends and internet access? What would be the best?

We've focused on boundaries with technology this week, but that isn't the only area where boundaries are needed. What are some other things that you indulge in, spend too much time with, allow too much of in your life? What are some other things that come to mind that you might need to withdraw from or set limits with?

> **A person without self-control is like a city with broken-down walls.**
>
> **PROVERBS 25:28 NLT**

How does this verse connect to or support what you've learned about setting your own boundaries this week?

 Pray about it . . .

- Tell God about any struggles you have with setting boundaries for technology (or other things).

- Ask God to show you if you are looking to those things to pass time or fight loneliness or hide from unhappiness.

- Admit to him anything that doesn't feel right about those things.

- Ask him to help you set healthy boundaries and to meet the needs you're using those things to fulfill.

- Thank Jesus for coming to this earth as a human so that you can learn how to handle things in your life by seeing how he lived his.

You Are Loved and Prayed Over

It has been a joy to write this book for you. And can I let you in on a secret? In some form or another, I have needed every single lesson I wrote about in this book. Today. That's the thing about being a Christian—it never ends. You don't get a plaque for years of service. You never outgrow God's love or your need for his grace. You don't graduate from Be Like Jesus University and move on to the next level.

This being-a-Christian thing? It's a lifelong journey of loving our Lord.

I can't thank you enough for letting me be a part of your journey. You have been prayed over countless times as I wrote this book, and now I want to share my final prayer for you.

Father God,

Thank you for this girl. Thank you for her desire to know you better and get closer to you.

Lord, I ask that you protect her. Protect her from the devil and all the ways he wants to distract her. Protect her from the world that tries to lead her away from you. God, give her strength and courage. Help her to be bold enough to follow you and humble enough to know you are her strength. God, send her friends who will support her and love her—friends who love you first.

Thank you for the work you have done in her heart and soul this year. I pray that she continues to become more like Jesus every day forward. Thank you for forgiving her for the times she has sinned and for the mistakes she will make in the future. Help her understand your grace and forgiveness and to know that she can never be separated from your love.

God, walk with her over these next few years as she discovers who you have made her to be. Lead her as she takes hold of her own faith and continues to develop her personal relationship with you. Put people in her life who will encourage and build her up, people who will point her to you and who will love her like you do.

Thank you for the time we got to spend together through the pages of this book. May you continue to bless her, make your face shine upon her, be gracious to her, turn your face toward her, and give her your peace.

In Jesus's name,
Amen.

Acknowledgments

Ben, thank you for your endless support, for pushing me, and for believing in me more than I believe in myself. I am so proud to be your wife.

Alayna, Camden, Kemper, Jayla, Brigg, and Glavin, you make me want to be more like Jesus. I pray that the lessons in this book come alive in our home and that you all grow up to be young men and women who love Jesus.

Mom and Dad, thank you for being a constant force of love and support. Tony and Connie, thank you for your prayers and for opening your home as my writing space. To my brothers, sisters-in-law, brothers-in-law, aunts, and uncles, your support has meant so very much to me.

Coffee friends, thank you for praying for me and this project since before it became a reality. Your support and willingness to love on my little boys while I wrote made this book possible.

God orchestrates countless little details as he weaves together his master plan. Lauren, Jenny, Mikala, Jen, Jillian, Carolyn, Leslie, Casey, Emily, and the Her View From Home writing community, you are the supporting details in my story.

Keely and Jennifer, thank you for believing in me and the messages God laid on my heart. Your wisdom and guidance have been irreplaceable. I appreciate your patience and encouragement—I didn't walk a single step on this first-time-author road alone. Thank you for that.

To Stephanie and the entire team at Bethany House, thank you for your mission to help readers deepen their faith. It has been a joy to work with you.

Father God, thank you for showing up time and time again throughout this entire process. You are so, so good.

Decision-Making Flowchart

When Facing Temptation, Ask God for HELP

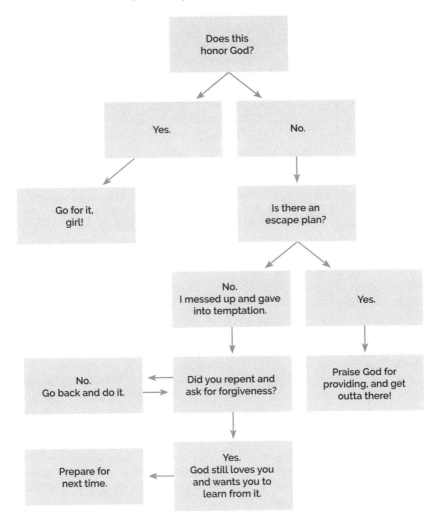

Does this honor God?

Yes. → Go for it, girl!

No. → Is there an escape plan?

No. I messed up and gave into temptation.

Yes. → Praise God for providing, and get outta there!

Did you repent and ask for forgiveness?

No. Go back and do it.

Yes. God still loves you and wants you to learn from it.

Prepare for next time.

Notes

Week 5 And It Was Good

1. "What Is a Mosquito?" Centers for Disease Control and Prevention, accessed March 5, 2020, last reviewed June 28, 2023, https://www.cdc.gov/mosquitoes/about/what-is-a-mosquito.html.

Week 8 I Can Be Confident because of What God Says about Me

1. Olivia Evans, Korin Miller, and Addison Aloian, "Taylor Swift's Total Net Worth in 2023: Her Eras Tour Tickets, Film, Merch, and More," *Women's Health*, August 10, 2023, updated November 17, 2023, https://www.womenshealthmag.com/life/a41690529/taylor-swift-net-worth/.

Week 11 Complaining Is Easier Than Complimenting

1. *Strong's Greek Concordance*, BibleHub.com, s.v. "4550. sapros," September 3, 2023, https://biblehub.com/greek/4550.htm.

Week 23 Do You Know What She Did? I Can't Forgive That.

1. Andy Andrews, *The Traveler's Gift* (Nashville: Thomas Nelson, 2002), 130–131.
2. Andy Andrews, *The Traveler's Gift* (Nashville: Thomas Nelson, 2002), 132.

Week 24 Saying I'm Sorry Isn't Enough

1. *Strong's Greek Concordance*, BibleHub.com, s.v. "3340. metanoeó," June 29, 2023, https://biblehub.com/greek/3340.htm.

Week 29 Is Satan Real?

1. Priscilla Shirer, *The Armor of God* (Nashville: Lifeway Press, 2015), 11.

Week 39 Is Prince Charming Out There? And Other Questions about Dating.

1. *Merriam-Webster*, s.v. "charm (*n*.)," last updated June 26, 2023, https://www.merriam-webster.com/dictionary/charm.

Week 49 God Tells the Ocean Waves Where to Stop

1. National Oceanic and Atmospheric Administration, "How long is the U.S. shoreline?" *National Ocean Service*, last updated August 8, 2023, https://oceanservice.noaa.gov/facts/shorelength.html.

KELSEY SCISM is a mother of six, wife, author, speaker, and most importantly a Christian loving our Lord. As a former language arts teacher, she loved inspiring and encouraging her students. Today, she finds inspiration in the everyday moments as a stay-at-home mom and hopes to encourage others along the way. She and her family live in a tiny town in Kansas.

Kelsey shares the countless lessons God is teaching her on her blog, *Loving Our Lord,* and can be found online here:

LovingOurLord.com

 @LovingOurLordwithKelseyScism

 @Kelsey.Scism

Words to Take with You

God determines my worth.
I am fearfully and wonderfully made.

God loves me so much he sent
his only Son to die for me.

He says that even when I feel alone,
he is with me.

God doesn't wonder what if,
he knows what will be.

God loves me . . .
I'm going to be okay.

God has protected me through
hard things before, and he is with me now.

God gives me strength and courage
when I feel weak and afraid.